Betty Crocker's
DO-AHEAD COOKBOOK

Betty Crocker's

DO-AHEAD COOKBOOK

MACMILLAN • USA

MACMILLAN
A Prentice Hall Macmillan Company
15 Columbus Circle
New York, New York 10023

Copyright © 1994 by General Mills, Inc., Minneapolis, Minnesota

MACMILLAN is a registered trademark of Macmillan, Inc.
BETTY CROCKER and BISQUICK are registered trademarks of General Mills, Inc.

Library of Congress Cataloging-in-Publication Data
Crocker, Betty
[Do-ahead cookbook]
Betty Crocker's do-ahead cookbook—Rev. Ed.
        p.   cm.
Includes index.
ISBN 0-02-860030-4
1. Cookery (Frozen foods)   2. Cold storage.   3. Make-ahead cookery   I. Title.
II: Title: Do-Ahead Cookbook.
TX828.C7   1995   641.6'153—dc20

CIP
94-12064
GENERAL MILLS, INC.
Betty Crocker Food and Publications Center
Director: Marcia Copeland
Editor: Jean E. Kozar
Recipe Development: Liz Woolever
Food Stylists: Katie McElroy, Carol Grones
Nutrition Department
Nutritionist: Elyse A. Cohen, M.S.
Photographic Services
Photographer: Nancy Doonan Dixon

Designed by Levavi & Levavi

Manufactured in the United States of America

10 9 8 7 6 5 4 3 2 1

First Edition
Front cover: Turkey-Chili Enchiladas (page 62); White Chocolate-Pecan Cheesecake (page 152)
Back cover: Chocolate Chip–Peanut Frozen Yogurt (page 160)

◧◧◧ Contents ◧◧◧

⊠⊠⊠ Introduction ⊠⊠⊠

We all are looking for ways to add more hours to the day. While we can't add more time, we can make it seem as if we have with a bit of creative organization. And that's the driving force behind this cookbook, using our time more effectively, and thereby liberating ourselves from the clock! The concept of "time-shifting" has become familiar to us by using the VCR to tape shows then viewing them when it's convenient. Well, this cookbook works much the same way—cook when you have the time, then serve when you'd like.

You'll find these recipes endlessly useful, whether you want to prepare part of a meal the night before, or would like to have a well-stocked freezer that lets you be ready for almost every occasion. And to ensure that your recipes stay fresh and appetizing, we have included complete information for wrapping and storing your do-ahead dishes.

The first chapter gives you great ideas for stress-free brunches, from savory Dilled Chicken-Leek Strata to luscious Overnight Pecan Rolls. Next there are easy main dishes that are perfect for any night of the week, such as Mexicali Steak, Italian Chicken Rolls and Lamb Cassoulet.

You'll appreciate the next chapter of menus for all occasions, from a holiday dinner to a backyard barbecue. Not only will you find do-ahead recipes, you'll appreciate having the menu planned for you.

Finally, there are wonderful desserts and appetizers that make the beginning or ending of any meal special! Doing these ahead makes them perfect for parties, or casual gatherings—it's always handy to have snacks ready. Enticing Five-Spice Chicken Wings or Savory Cappuccino Cake Roll, Pecan Pie or Three-Nut Baklava ready and waiting means you can have wonderful treats any time you'd like.

We think once you've tried do-ahead cooking, you'll be hooked! You'll find that with the help of Betty Crocker, it's possible to find more time in the day, and still enjoy delicious, home-cooked meals!

The Betty Crocker Editors

⬚⬚⬚ Chilling Out ⬚⬚⬚

Busy schedules make do-ahead foods and meals attractive anytime. With a little planning and recipes that adapt well to advance preparation, foods can be ready whenever they're needed. Your best friends for do-ahead preparation are your refrigerator and freezer. They work 24 hours a day to keep perishable food safe to eat by keeping fresh foods chilled and other foods frozen for longer storage. See the Cold Storage Chart, page 165.

Refrigerator storage is basically quite easy. Just remember to cover foods or wrap them tightly before refrigerating. Since most people have many more questions about what can be frozen and how to do it, most of our tips focus on freezing. You'll find this information helpful and can easily become a freezer expert!

SIX KEYS TO SUCCESSFUL DO-AHEAD FREEZING

We think you'll find these tips so helpful that you'll even want to pass them on to family and friends.

1. Prepare and Cook

• Plan to prepare and cook only high quality foods for freezing. Freezing can keep flavor, color and texture, but cannot improve on original food quality.
• Use safe handling food practices during preparation, cooking and freezing. See Tips for Safe Food Handling, page 13.
• Use the refrigerator or the ice water method (below) to cool foods quickly. To avoid bacterial growth, do not let perishable foods stand at room temperature to cool.

2. Cool Quickly

Once food is cooked, cool it quickly to warm (about 100°F.) before freezing to retain the best quality and flavor. The slower food freezes, the larger the ice crystals are, which makes the food mushy when thawed. A quantity of hot food added to a freezer makes the freezer work harder, creates moisture and also can partially thaw already frozen foods. Cooling the food down quickly before freezing is especially important for moist foods such as soups, stews and sauces. The amount of time it takes to cool food quickly depends on the kind and quantity of food. Regardless of quantity, stir the food every 15 minutes. Here are several methods you can use to cool food quickly:

• Refrigerate food uncovered in a shallow container (less than 2 inches deep). Use two for large food quantities.
• Carefully transfer food from the cooking pan into a large shallow pan such as a cake pan or roasting pan in a sink partially filled with ice and water.
• Refrigerate perishable foods such as those including meats, eggs, dairy products, fruits or vegetables until ready to freeze. Do not let these foods stand at room temperature to cool before freezing.

3. Pack It Up!

Your supermarket and other stores provide many options for freezer packaging:
• Use airtight, moisture-vaporproof containers and materials specifically designed for food storage that can withstand freezer temperatures of 0°F. and below.
• See Easy Guide to Freezer Packaging (page 12).
• Properly package foods for best results. Allow about ¼- to ½-inch headspace for expansion, especially important for chunky soups, stews and sauces.

Be sure to label all packages and containers before freezing.

4. Airtight Is Right!

If you've seen dry discolored surfaces on frozen foods, you're familiar with "freezer burn." Unprotected exposure to cold air shortens storage life and impairs quality and flavor. Pack food tightly with the container almost full to eliminate as much air as possible.
• "Shrink-wrap" foods packaged in freezer bags with either of these methods:

Press out as much air as possible before sealing. Close the bag except for a ½-inch opening. Insert a drinking straw and suck out any remaining air until the bag "shrinks" around the food. Quickly slip out the straw and seal the bag completely.

Press out as much air as possible before sealing. Close the bag except for a ½-inch opening. Submerge the filled bag in a container of water, pushing the air out of the bag; seal the bag.
• When freezing foods in a container where the lid or wrap is over ¼-inch above the surface of the food, place aluminum foil or plastic wrap directly on the top of the food before covering to seal out the air. Remove before baking, carefully using a hot wet towel to help release the foil if necessary.
• See Airtight Ways to Wrap, page 11.

5. Freeze with Ease

• Adding unfrozen food can significantly increase the temperature of the freezer. To maintain ideal freezing temperatures and efficiency, do not freeze more than about ¹⁄₁₀ of the capacity of the freezer at one time or freezing will be slow. Set the thermostat to −10° to speed freezing; once the food is frozen (usually 24 hours), reset the temperature to 0°.
• Allow space around the food for the air to circulate.
• When freezing several packages at once, place them in a single layer in the coldest part of the freezer directly on the freezer shelf, leaving space between for air circulation, until solidly frozen. Once frozen, the packages can be stacked.
• To quick-freeze foods, arrange in a single layer, not touching, on a cookie sheet or jelly roll pan. Freeze uncovered or covered with an inverted cake pan until solid (12 to 24 hours). Package and freeze so smaller amounts can be used as needed.
• Purchase wire baskets to place in your freezer to help keep it organized and designate each for certain types of food.

YOU REALLY CAN FREEZE THESE FOODS!

Here is a collection of many foods you may not have thought about freezing. They will keep best if used within 3 to 6 months.

- **Bananas**—ripe in their skins but unable to be used right away. Thaw each 30 to 60 seconds in the microwave and use in baked foods. Frozen bananas can also be eaten as a treat.
- **Bread crumbs**—buttered or plain
- **Candied fruits**—such as fruitcake mix
- **Coconut**—grated fresh or purchased
- **Coffee, beans or ground**—package in small amounts to avoid repeated exposure to air. Or freeze leftover brewed coffee in ice cube trays for adding to iced coffee or for extra added flavor to gravies or sauces
- **Cranberries**—freeze them when in season and use year round
- **Dried fruits**—such as apples, apricots, dates and raisins
- **Flavored butters**—reshape into blocks; refrigerate until firm. Cut into small amounts and freeze in a single layer; package when frozen.

- **Flour**—especially in hot, humid weather or if not frequently used
- **Herbs and spices, dried**—flavors keep longer in the freezer. Fresh herb sprigs and leaves can be frozen but will become limp; chop while frozen and use in cooked recipes.
- **Melon**—leftover chunks can be frozen, then used in fruit drinks
- **Nuts**—shelled or unshelled
- **Orange or lemon peel**—fresh grated or finely shredded
- **Pasta and rice, cooked or uncooked**—texture of cooked pasta may change slightly; freezing dry pasta in hot, humid weather can help prevent bugs
- **Pesto, soup stock or spaghetti sauce**—freeze in ice cube trays for quick and easy flavor additions to your recipes
- **Seeds**—such as poppyseed, pumpkin, sesame and sunflower
- **Tea, loose or in bags**—or leftover brewed tea in ice cube trays for adding to iced tea or punch

PLEASE DO NOT FREEZE THESE FOODS!

Some foods are not recommended for freezing because the quality of the thawed product is poor.

- **Cooked egg whites** become tough
- **Crackers and chips** absorb moisture
- **Cream, custard or meringue-topped pies** will separate and lose texture quality
- **Crumb toppings** on casseroles and desserts can become soggy. Add the topping before baking.

- **Egg-white frostings and meringues for pies** shrink and become tough
- **Mayonnaise or salad dressings** may separate
- **Salad greens** become soggy
- **Raw apples and grapes** become mushy, though some people find *frozen* grapes a refreshing snack.
- **Raw tomatoes** will become limp and watery, but can be frozen for use in cooking (reduce amounts of added liquid)

6. Heat and Serve

• Follow the directions in the recipes for heating and serving. Remember not to leave hot foods at room temperature for more than 2 hours, including preparation time.
• To heat and serve your own favorite recipes, find a similar recipe and use the directions as a guideline. Make some notes for future reference.

WRAP IT UP!

Keeping food the freshest for any length of time depends, in part, on good packaging containers, wrapping materials and a few extra minutes of time.

For the Freezer

• Freezer wraps and containers should be airtight, moistureproof and vaporproof. These materials retain the moisture in the food and help prevent freezer burn.
• Good materials are heavy-duty aluminum foil, heavy-weight plastic wrap and airtight freezer bags or containers. See Easy Guide to Freezer Packaging, page 12.
• Remove as much air as possible from containers when freezing foods.

• More delicate foods, such as decorated cakes, certain types of cookies or popovers, may need to be put in a box or sturdy container for protection. Wrap the food, then place it in a box or container.

Wearing the Right Label

• Be sure to label all packages and containers before freezing—frozen foods sometimes have a tendency to get lost in the freezer, and it's not easy to remember all the details about each item after they've been there awhile!
• Label package sides for an upright freezer and package tops for a chest-type freezer.
• Include the following information: name of recipe, storage time ("use before" date), number of servings and any directions for reheating or preparing after freezing.
• Use freezer labels or freezer tape designed to stick at very cold temperatures. Many freezer bags and rigid containers already include a special place for writing—take advantage of this convenience! Mark with a ballpoint pen, crayon or waterproof felt-tipped pen.

AIRTIGHT WAYS TO WRAP

These are the best ways to wrap foods airtight using ample squares or rectangles of heavy-duty aluminum foil or freezer wrap:

The Drugstore Wrap—best for meat, poultry and fish

1. Place the food in the center of a large piece of wrap. Use crumpled foil to pad sharp corners or bones. Bring the long sides of wrap together over the food and fold to secure.

2. Fold down in about 1-inch folds, pressing air out until snug against the food. Fold over the short ends at least twice.

The Casserole Wrap—best for casseroles of any type

1. Turn the baking pan or casserole upside down and mold a sheet of heavy-duty aluminum foil over it, leaving a 1½-inch collar. Turn the pan over and press in the molded lining. Fill the pan.

2. Cover the food directly with another sheet of foil the size of the pan with the foil collar. Press out the air from the center. Fold the edges over at least twice to seal.

The Bundle Wrap—best for foods with unusual shapes

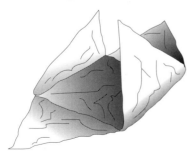

1. Place the food in the center of a large piece of heavy-duty aluminum foil. Bring all four corners up to the top center in the shape of a pyramid.

2. Fold all the edges that meet over at least twice to seal, pressing out the air until the foil is snug against the food.

EASY GUIDE TO FREEZER PACKAGING

CONTAINERS	TYPE OF STORAGE*	HELPFUL TIPS
Shapely Rigid Classics		
• Glass, ceramic or stoneware casseroles with lids	• Long term	—Use only glass containers that are labeled as safe for freezing
• Wide-mouthed freezer jars	• Long term	—Line casseroles with heavy-duty aluminum foil (see The Casserole Wrap, page 11).
• Rigid plastic freezer containers with lids	• Long term	After freezing solid, remove food from casserole so it can be used during the time the food is frozen. Return the frozen food to the casserole before baking.
• Metal baking pans and glass baking dishes	• Long term	
• Aluminum foil pans	• Long term	
• Reusable plastic food containers	• Short term	
Bags and Boxes		
• Heavy-duty food storage freezer bags	• Long term	—Available sizes range from 1 pint to 2 gallons
• Heat-sealed plastic food storage bags	• Long term	—Heat-sealed bags freeze up to 1 quart of food
• Plastic food storage bags	• Short-term	—Always label bags *before* adding food.
• Plastic bags (produce, etc.)	• Not recommended	—When adding moist foods such as chili to plastic bags with zipper tops, for a clean seal, fold the top down about 2 inches and place in a bowl for support.
• Paper bags	• Temporary	
• Freezer boxes	• Long term	
• Cardboard boxes (such as cereal boxes, milk cartons or cake boxes)	• To hold freezer bags so they easily stack or protect delicate foods from crushing	
Wraps		
• Heavy-duty aluminum foil	• Long term	—See Airtight Ways to Wrap, page 11
• Freezer paper	• Long term	—Check labels—not all wraps are recommended for freezer storage.
• Aluminum foil	• Short term	

*Long term = over 1 month; Short term = up to 1 month; Temporary = up to 1 week.

• Heavy plastic wrap • Waxed paper • Parchment paper	• Short term • Temporary • Temporary	—Do not use waxed paper, regular foil or parchment paper as the only wrap. —Delicate foods, such as rolled cookies or popovers, may need to be put in a box or sturdy container for protection. Wrap the food and then place in a box or rigid container to avoid crushing.
Freezer Tape		
	• Tape-wrapped • Seal lids to casseroles and plastic containers	—Withstands colder temperatures than regular masking or cellophane tape. —Tape around lids, over entire seam to seal out air.

TIPS FOR SAFE FOOD HANDLING

• Keep hot foods hot (above 140°) and cold foods cold (below 40°).
• Most food poisoning bacteria don't grow at refrigerator or freezer temperatures, but thrive at room temperatures (60° to 90°) and can't be seen, smelled or tasted.
• Don't allow hot or cold foods to remain at room temperature for more than 2 hours, including preparation time.
• Keep preparation areas and hands clean, washing with soap and water often. Refrigerate leftovers immediately at 40°F or below to inhibit the growth of bacteria and keep no longer than 48 hours.
• Freezing foods at 0° or below can stop bacterial growth but will not kill bacteria that are already present.
• Thoroughly reheat foods to an internal temperature of 165°F or above.

THAWING FROZEN FOODS

• Many foods can be cooked from the frozen state and need not be thawed before cooking. Some meats and poultry must be thawed before cooking. The best way to thaw is in the refrigerator. Or, thaw in the microwave according to the manufacturer's directions.
• Meats and poultry may be safely frozen only twice—once when fresh, and once after cooking. Refrigerate meats to cool quickly, then cut into meal-sized amounts or slices for freezing.
• Thawed fish and seafood should never be refrozen.
• Cakes should be thawed on a cake rack while still wrapped.

MICROWAVE FOR EASY REHEATING

Busy schedules often make only 1 or 2 servings necessary at meal times. The microwave is the most convenient way to reheat smaller amounts of already-cooked foods. Since microwave ovens vary, the chart below gives *approximate* heating times.

- Place food in microwavable utensils
- Use High power except as noted
- Cover foods for fastest heating using a lid, waxed paper or vented plastic wrap
- Stir, rearrange or rotate food after half the reheating time; stir before serving
- Check food at minimum heating time

MICROWAVE REHEATING CHART		
TYPE OF FOOD	**REFRIGERATED**	**FROZEN**
Plate of Food (casserole plus vegetable or sliced meat plus 2 vegetables)	2 to 4 minutes	6 to 9 minutes
Soups, Stews or Saucy Main Dishes		
1 to 2 cups	3 to 5 minutes	5 to 11 minutes Medium-High (70%)
2 to 4 cups	4 to 7 minutes	11 to 18 minutes Medium-High (70%)
Layered Main Dish Casseroles (lasagne)		Let stand a few minutes after heating
1 serving (3 × 4 inches)	4 to 6 minutes Medium-High (70%)	5 to 8 minutes Medium-High (70%)
2 servings (2 inches apart)	5 to 9 minutes Medium-High (70%)	9 to 14 minutes Medium-High (70%)
Vegetables, cut up		
½ to 1 cup	1 to 2 minutes	2 to 4 minutes
1 to 2 cups	2 to 3 minutes	3 to 6 minutes

NUTRITION AND TESTING INFORMATION FOR RECIPES

Nutritional information Per Serving is provided at the end of each recipe in this book. Besides Calories, the nutrients calculated include Protein, Carbohydrate (incuding Dietary Fiber), Fat (including Unsaturated and Saturated), Cholesterol and Sodium. The percentages of U.S. Recommended Daily Allowances (RDA) have also been calculated for Vitamins A and C, Calcium and Iron.

• When an ingredient choice is given, such as ⅓ cup plain yogurt or sour cream, the first ingredient listed was used for nutritional calculation.

• When ingredient ranges or more than one serving size is indicated, the first weight or serving is used to calculate nutritional information.

• Ingredients referred to as "if desired" are not included in the nutrition calculations, whether mentioned in the ingredient listing or in the recipe text as a suggestion.

• An asterisk (*) in the nutrition information indicates that the recipe contains less than 2% U.S. RDA of those nutrients.

• For recipe testing and nutrition calculations, large eggs, 2% milk and regular stick margarine (not tub or whipped) were used. No low-fat or nonfat ingredients were used unless stated in the recipe.

• Cookware and bakeware without nonstick coatings was used for recipe testing. Solid vegetable shortening was used to grease pans unless otherwise stated. A portable electric hand mixer was used for mixing only when mixer speeds are given in the recipe.

1

Ready-Ahead Best Bets for Brunch

Chicken-Leek Strata (page 22)

Mushroom Quiche

Like a more traditional quiche? Just omit the mushrooms and the pimiento. We pour the filling in the shell with the pie pan already on the oven rack. It's a great way to prevent spills—but be sure your oven rack slides smoothly!

*Pastry for 9-inch One-Crust Pie
    (see page 149)*
*8 slices bacon, crisply cooked and
    crumbled*
*1 can (4 ounces) mushroom stems and
    pieces, drained*
*1 jar (2 ounces) diced pimientos, well
    drained*
1 cup shredded Swiss cheese (4 ounces)
⅓ cup finely chopped onion
4 eggs
2 cups whipping (heavy) cream
¼ teaspoon salt
¼ teaspoon pepper
⅛ teaspoon ground red pepper (cayenne)

Prepare pastry. Ease into quiche dish, 9 × 1½ inches, or pie plate, 9 × 1¼ inches. Sprinkle bacon, mushrooms, pimientos, cheese and onion in pastry-lined dish. Beat eggs slightly in medium bowl. Beat in remaining ingredients. STOP HERE—see **To Store** and **To Cook**.

To serve now, heat oven to 425°. Place pastry-lined dish with layered ingredients on oven rack. Pour egg mixture into dish. Bake 15 minutes. Reduce oven temperature to 300°. Bake about 30 minutes longer or until knife inserted in center comes out clean. Let stand 10 minutes before cutting. *6 servings.*

Per Serving: Calories 650; Protein 16 g; Carbohydrate 22g (Dietary Fiber 1g); Fat 56 g (Unsaturated 29 g, Saturated 27 g); Cholesterol 270 mg; Sodium 510 mg. Percent of U.S. RDA: Vitamin A 36%; Vitamin C 10%; Calcium 24%; Iron 10%.

To Store

Refrigerator: Cover pastry-lined dish with layered ingredients tightly, cover egg mixture tightly and refrigerate no longer than 24 hours.

To Cook from Refrigerator

Oven: About 1¼ hours before serving, heat oven to 425°. Uncover pastry-lined dish and place on oven rack. Stir egg mixture and pour into dish. Bake 15 minutes. Reduce oven temperature to 300°. Bake 30 to 40 minutes longer or until knife inserted in center comes out clean.

Cheddar-Egg-Rice Bake

1 cup sliced mushrooms (about 3 ounces)
1 medium onion, chopped (about ½ cup)
⅔ cup uncooked regular long grain rice
1⅓ cups water
1 cup frozen chopped broccoli
1 cup small curd creamed cottage cheese
¾ cup shredded Cheddar cheese
   (3 ounces)
2 tablespoons dry bread crumbs
1 tablespoon chopped fresh or 1 teaspoon
   dried basil leaves
¼ teaspoon salt
¼ teaspoon pepper
2 eggs, beaten

To Complete Recipe:
   ¼ cup shredded Cheddar cheese (1
      ounce)

Lightly grease quiche dish, 9 × ½ inch, or pie plate, 9 × ¼ inch. Mix mushrooms, onion, rice and water in 3-quart saucepan. Heat to boiling; reduce heat. Cover and simmer about 20 minutes, stirring occasionally, until rice is tender. Stir in broccoli and cottage cheese. Stir in remaining ingredients except ¼ cup Cheddar cheese. STOP HERE—see **To Store** and **To Cook.**

To complete recipe and serve now, heat oven to 325°. Bake 40 minutes. Sprinkle with ¼ cup Cheddar cheese. Bake 10 to 15 minutes longer or until center is hot. Let stand 5 minutes before cutting. *6 servings.*

Per Serving: Calories 235; Protein 14 g; Carbohydrate 24 g (Dietary Fiber 2 g); Fat 10 g (Unsaturated 4 g, Saturated 6 g); Cholesterol 95 mg; Sodium 390 mg. Percent of U.S. RDA: Vitamin A 10%; Vitamin C 6%; Calcium 14%; Iron 10%.

To Store

Refrigerator: Cover unbaked casserole tightly and refrigerate no longer than 24 hours.

To Cook from Refrigerator

Oven: About 1¼ hours before serving, heat oven to 325°. Uncover and bake 50 minutes. Sprinkle with ¼ cup Cheddar cheese. Bake 10 to 15 minutes longer or until center is hot.

Herbed Biscuit-Beef Bake

½ pound ground beef
1 medium onion, chopped (about ½ cup)
1½ teaspoons chopped fresh or ½
　　teaspoon dried oregano leaves
1½ teaspoons chopped fresh or ½
　　teaspoon dried basil leaves
¼ teaspoon fennel seed
¼ teaspoon pepper
1 cup shredded Monterey Jack cheese
　　with jalapeño chilis or plain Monterey
　　Jack cheese (4 ounces)
½ cup Bisquick® Original baking mix
¼ teaspoon salt
2 eggs
1 cup milk

Heat oven to 400°. Cook ground beef and onion in 10-inch skillet over medium heat, stirring frequently, until beef is brown; drain well. Stir in oregano, basil, fennel seed and pepper. Divide beef mixture among four 10-ounce custard cups or 8-ounce soufflé dishes. Sprinkle with cheese. Mix remaining ingredients; pour over cheese. Cover cups with aluminum foil and bake 10 minutes. Uncover and bake about 15 minutes longer or until crust is golden. See **TO STORE** and **TO REHEAT**. Can be served now. *4 servings.*

Per Serving: Calories 355; Protein 22 g; Carbohydrate 16 g (Dietary Fiber 1 g); Fat 23 g (Unsaturated 12 g, Saturated 11 g); Cholesterol 170 mg; Sodium 620 mg. Percent of U.S. RDA: Vitamin A 16%; Vitamin C *; Calcium 32%; Iron 12%.

TO STORE

Freezer: Cool baked casseroles 30 minutes. Wrap tightly with aluminum foil and label. Freeze no longer than 2 months.

TO REHEAT FROM FREEZER

Oven: About 1 hour before serving, heat oven to 350°. Bake covered casseroles 20 minutes. Uncover and bake 25 to 30 minutes longer or until hot.

Herbed Biscuit-Beef Bake

Herbed Biscuit
Beef Bake 9/22
© 1992 General Mills, Inc.

Chicken-Leek Strata

Refrigerating this easy strata overnight ensures that the bread soaks up all the egg and milk mixture, creating an enticingly moist dish.

1 tablespoon margarine or butter
1 cup sliced leek
8 slices French bread, each ½ inch thick
1 cup chopped cooked chicken or turkey
1 tablespoon chopped fresh or 1 teaspoon dried dill weed
2 cups shredded mozzarella cheese (8 ounces)
4 eggs, beaten
2 cups milk
½ teaspoon salt
¼ teaspoon pepper

Heat margarine in 1-quart saucepan until melted. Cook leek in margarine over medium heat about 3 minutes, stirring frequently, until softened; remove from heat. Cut enough bread into 1-inch pieces to measure 5 cups. Mix bread pieces, leek, chicken and dill weed. Spread bread mixture in ungreased square baking dish, 8 × 8 × 2 inches. Sprinkle with cheese. Mix remaining ingredients; pour over cheese. See **To Store** and **To Cook.** *6 servings.*

Per Serving: Calories 345; Protein 27 g; Carbohydrate 26 g (Dietary Fiber 7 g); Fat 15 g (Unsaturated 8 g, Saturated 7 g); Cholesterol 190 mg; Sodium 700 mg. Percent of U.S. RDA: Vitamin A 18%; Vitamin C 0%; Calcium 44%; Iron 12%.

To Store

Refrigerator: Cover tightly and refrigerate at least 4 hours but no longer than 24 hours.

To Cook from Refrigerator

Oven: About 1¼ hours before serving, heat oven to 325°. Uncover and bake 50 to 55 minutes or until knife inserted in center comes out clean. Let stand 10 minutes before cutting.

Spicy Sausage-Vegetable Strata

1 pound spicy or hot bulk pork sausage
1 medium onion, chopped (about ½ cup)
1 loaf French bread (about 10 inches),
    cut into ¾-inch slices
½ cup roasted bell peppers (from 7.25-
    ounce jar), cut into ¼-inch strips*
2 medium zucchini, thinly sliced (about 2
    cups)
6 eggs
¾ cup ricotta cheese
2 cups milk
½ cup grated Parmesan cheese

Cook sausage and onion in 10-inch skillet over medium heat, stirring occasionally, until sausage is no longer pink; drain well. Arrange bread slices in rectangular baking dish, 11 × 7 × 1½ inches, cutting to fit if necessary. Spread sausage mixture over bread. Top with bell peppers and zucchini. Beat eggs and ricotta cheese in medium bowl until blended. Stir in milk. Pour over mixture in baking dish. Sprinkle with Parmesan cheese. See **TO STORE** and **TO COOK**. *8 servings.*

*To roast fresh bell peppers: Broil peppers with tops about 5 inches from heat, turning occasionally, until skin is evenly blistered and lightly browned. Place peppers in a plastic bag and close tightly. Let stand 20 minutes. Remove skin, stems, seeds and membranes from peppers.

Per Serving: Calories 420; Protein 23 g; Carbohydrate 44 g (Dietary Fiber 3 g); Fat 17 g (Unsaturated 10 g, Saturated 7 g); Cholesterol 200 mg; Sodium 910 mg. Percent of U.S. RDA: Vitamin A 16%; Vitamin C 6%; Calcium 32%; Iron 20%.

TO STORE

Refrigerator: Cover tightly and refrigerate at least 2 hours but no longer than 24 hours.

TO COOK FROM REFRIGERATOR

Oven: About 1 hour before serving, heat oven to 350°. Uncover pan and bake 45 to 55 minutes or until top is puffed and center is set. Serve immediately.

Shrimp and Cheese Crepes

Small shrimp, sometimes sold as salad shrimp, are just the right size for this dish. You can bake the crepes in a rectangular pan or baking dish that's 13 × 9 × 2 inches, but the crepes will have a softer texture.

Crepes (see page 154)
1 tablespoon grated Parmesan cheese
1 cup ricotta cheese
1 cup shredded Swiss cheese (4 ounces)
12 ounces cooked small shrimp
2 medium stalks celery, thinly sliced
*   (about 1 cup)*
½ cup sliced green onions (about 5
*   medium)*
⅛ teaspoon ground nutmeg

To Complete Recipe:
¼ cup grated Parmesan cheese

Prepare Crepes—except substitute 1 tablespoon Parmesan cheese for the sugar and omit the vanilla. Grease jelly roll pan, 15½ × 10½ × 1 inch. (If planning to freeze, use ungreased cookie sheet.) Mix ricotta cheese and Swiss cheese in medium bowl until blended. Stir in shrimp, celery, onions and nutmeg. Spoon shrimp mixture onto 1 side of each crepe. Roll up. Place filled crepes, seam sides down, in pan. STOP HERE—see **To Store** and **To Cook.**

To complete recipe and serve now, heat oven to 350°. Cover with aluminum foil and bake 20 minutes. Sprinkle with ¼ cup Parmesan cheese. Bake uncovered 5 to 10 minutes longer or until hot. *6 servings.*

> **Per Serving:** Calories 405; Protein 32 g; Carbohydrate 33 g (Dietary Fiber 2 g); Fat 17 g (Unsaturated 9 g, Saturated 8 g); Cholesterol 220 mg; Sodium 460 mg. Percent of U.S. RDA: Vitamin A 24%; Vitamin C 2%; Calcium 52%; Iron 22%.

To Store

Refrigerator: Cover unbaked crepes tightly with aluminum foil and refrigerate no longer than 48 hours.

Freezer: Freeze uncovered about 1 hour or until firm. Place crepes in labeled airtight freezer container. Freeze no longer than 2 weeks.

To Cook from Refrigerator

Oven: About 35 minutes before serving, heat oven to 350°. Bake in covered pan 20 minutes. Sprinkle with ¼ cup Parmesan cheese. Bake uncovered 5 to 10 minutes longer or until hot.

To Cook from Freezer

Oven: About 55 minutes before serving, heat oven to 375°. Grease jelly roll pan, 15½ × 10½ × 1 inch. Place crepes, seam sides down, in pan, making sure crepes do not touch. Cover with aluminum foil and bake 30 minutes. Sprinkle with ¼ cup Parmesan cheese. Bake uncovered about 15 minutes longer or until hot.

Shrimp and Cheese Crepes; Three-Fruit Medley (page 33)

Orange-stuffed French Toast

If you like, you can double—or even triple— this recipe so you can have plenty on hand for an easy breakfast or brunch.

8 slices French bread, each 1 inch thick
1 package (3 ounces) cream cheese,
*   softened*
¼ cup chopped pecans, toasted
3 tablespoons orange marmalade
3 eggs
2 tablespoons granulated sugar
½ teaspoon grated orange peel
½ cup orange juice
1 teaspoon vanilla

To Complete Recipe:
2 tablespoons margarine or butter
Powdered sugar or maple-flavored syrup,
*   if desired*

Cut a 3-inch pocket in each slice bread by cutting through the top crust. Mix cream cheese, pecans and marmalade. Spread about 1 tablespoon cream cheese mixture in each pocket. Mix eggs, granulated sugar, orange peel, orange juice, and vanilla. Dip bread into egg mixture, coating both sides. STOP HERE—see **To Store** and **To Cook.**

To complete recipe and serve now, heat griddle or skillet over medium heat or to 375°. Heat 1 tablespoon of the margarine in 10-inch skillet or griddle until bubbly. Cook 4 slices bread in margarine about 1½ minutes on each side or until golden. Repeat with remaining margarine and bread. Sprinkle with powdered sugar or serve with maple syrup. *4 servings.*

> **Per Serving:** Calories 500; Protein 13 g; Carbohydrate 62 g (Dietary Fiber 2 g); Fat 23 g (Unsaturated 16 g, Saturated 7 g); Cholesterol 180 mg; Sodium 590 mg. Percent of U.S. RDA: Vitamin A 20%; Vitamin C 6%; Calcium 10%; Iron 16%.

TO STORE

Freezer: Cover cookie sheet with waxed paper. Place egg-dipped bread slices on waxed paper. Freeze uncovered about 1 hour or until firm. Place bread in labeled airtight freezer container. Freeze no longer than 2 months.

TO COOK FROM FREEZER

Oven: About 20 minutes before serving, heat oven to 425°. Generously brush cookie sheet with margarine. Place bread on cookie sheet. Bake 6 minutes; turn. Bake 2 to 5 minutes longer or until golden. Sprinkle with powdered sugar or serve with maple syrup.

Orange-stuffed French Toast

Raised Pancakes

Here's any easy way to have pancake batter on hand, first thing in the morning, for that hungry gang. And with the addition of the yeast, the pancakes taste a little like sourdough.

> *1 package active active dry yeast*
> *¼ cup warm water (105° to 115°)*
> *1 egg*
> *1⅓ cups milk*
> *2 cups Bisquick® Original baking mix*

Dissolve yeast in warm water in large bowl. Add remaining ingredients; beat with hand beater until smooth. See **To Store** and **To Cook.** *Twenty 4-inch pancakes.*

Per Pancake: Calories 50; Protein 1g; Carbohydrate 7g (Dietary Fiber 0g); Fat 2g (Unsaturated 2g, Saturated 0g); Cholesterol 10mg; Sodium 170mg. Percent of U.S. RDA: Vitamin A *%; Vitamin C *%; Calcium 2%; Iron 2%.

To Store

Refrigerator: Cover tightly and refrigerate at least 8 hours but no longer than 24 hours.

To Cook from Refrigerator

Stovetop: About 20 minutes before serving, heat griddle or skillet over medium heat or to 375°. Grease griddle with oil if necessary. For each pancake, pour scant ¼ cup batter onto hot griddle. Cook pancakes until dry around edges and bubbles on top break. Turn and cook other sides until golden brown.

Cinnamon-Apple Toast

> *½ cup sugar*
> *¾ teaspoon ground cinnamon*
> *2 tablespoons margarine or butter, softened*
> *6 slices bread, toasted*
> *1 jar (15 ounces) chunky applesauce*
> *⅓ cup raisins*

Grease rectangular pan, 13 × 9 × 2 inches. Mix sugar and cinnamon; sprinkle 2 tablespoons into pan. Spread margarine on toast; place buttered side up in pan. Sprinkle 2 tablespoons of the sugar mixture evenly over toast. Spread applesauce on toast. Sprinkle with raisins. Sprinkle remaining sugar mixture over applesauce. See **To Store** and **To Cook.** *6 servings.*

Per Serving: Calories 250; Protein 2g; Carbohydrate 51g (Dietary Fiber 2g); Fat 5g (Unsaturated 4g, Saturated 1g); Cholesterol 0mg; Sodium 170mg. Percent of U.S. RDA: Vitamin A 4%; Vitamin C 0%; Calcium 4%; Iron 8%.

To Store

Refrigerator: Cover tightly and refrigerate at least 4 hours but no longer than 24 hours.

To Cook from Refrigerator

Oven: About 45 minutes before serving, heat oven to 350°. Uncover and bake about 35 minutes or until warm. Serve warm.

Hearty Hash Browns

*1 package (6 ounces) hash brown
   potatoes with onions*
Boiling water
*½ cup chopped green onions (about 5
   medium)*
*1 cup shredded sharp Cheddar cheese
   (4 ounces)*
¼ teaspoon salt
3 tablespoons margarine or butter

Pour enough boiling water over potatoes to
cover; let stand 5 minutes. Drain thoroughly.
Layer half each of the potatoes, onions and
cheese in ungreased square baking dish,
8 × 8 × 2 inches. Sprinkle with half of the salt;
dot with half of the margarine. Repeat with remaining ingredients. STOP HERE—see **To
Store** and **To Cook.**

To serve now, heat oven to 350°. Cover with
aluminum foil and bake 20 minutes. Uncover
and bake about 10 minutes longer or until edges
are golden brown and cheese is melted. *4 to 6
servings.*

Per Serving: Calories 305; Protein 8g; Carbohydrate 15g
(Dietary Fiber 1g); Fat 24g (Unsaturated 16g, Saturated 8g);
Cholesterol 30mg; Sodium 500mg. Percent of U.S. RDA:
Vitamin A 18%; Vitamin C 6%; Calcium 16%; Iron 2%.

To Store

Refrigerator: Cover unbaked hash browns
tightly with aluminum foil and refrigerate no
longer than 24 hours.

To Cook from Refrigerator

Oven: About 45 minutes before serving, heat
oven to 350°. Bake covered 20 minutes.
Uncover and bake about 15 minutes longer or
until edges are golden brown and cheese is
melted.

Buttery Streusel Coffee Cakes

Feel free to tailor the coffee cakes to fit your taste. When you make the brown sugar and nut filling, for each cake add ½ cup berries or chopped apples, or add ¼ cup dried fruit such as cherries or apricots. You'll love the variety!

Buttery Streusel Topping (right)
3 cups all-purpose flour
1 cup granulated sugar
1 tablespoon plus 2 teaspoons baking powder
1 teaspoon salt
⅓ cup vegetable oil
2 eggs
1¼ cups milk
½ cup packed brown sugar
½ cup finely chopped nuts
1 teaspoon ground cinnamon
Powdered Sugar Glaze (right), if desired

Heat oven to 375°. Grease 2 round pans, 9 × 1½ inches, or 2 square pans, 9 × 9 × 2 inches. Prepare Buttery Streusel Topping; reserve. Mix flour, granulated sugar, baking powder, salt, oil, eggs and milk until moistened; beat vigorously 30 seconds. Spread one-third of the batter (about 1⅓ cups) in each pan.

Mix brown sugar, nuts and cinnamon; sprinkle half of the mixture over batter in each pan. Spread half of the remaining batter (about ⅔ cup) over nut mixture in each pan. Sprinkle with topping. Bake 30 to 35 minutes or until toothpick inserted in center comes out clean. Cool on wire rack 30 minutes. Drizzle with Powdered Sugar Glaze. See **To Store** and **To Reheat.** Can be served now. *2 cakes, 8 servings each.*

BUTTERY STREUSEL TOPPING

¼ cup (½ stick) firm margarine or butter
1 cup sugar
½ cup all-purpose flour

Cut margarine into sugar and flour until crumbly.

POWDERED SUGAR GLAZE

2 cups powdered sugar
¼ cup (½ stick) margarine or butter, softened
1 teaspoon vanilla
⅓ to ½ cup water

Mix powdered sugar, margarine and vanilla in medium bowl. Stir in water, about 2 tablespoons at a time, until drizzling consistency.

Per Serving: Calories 430; Protein 5 g; Carbohydrate 70 g (Dietary Fiber 1 g); Fat 15 g (Unsaturated 12 g, Saturated 3 g); Cholesterol 30 mg; Sodium 350 mg. Percent of U.S. RDA: Vitamin A 10%; Vitamin C *; Calcium 12%; Iron 8%.

TO STORE

Freezer: Cool baked coffee cakes completely. Wrap tightly and label. Freeze no longer than 3 months.

TO REHEAT FROM FREEZER

Oven: About 25 minutes before serving, heat oven to 350°. Uncover and bake about 20 minutes or until warm. Serve warm.

Overnight Pecan Rolls

3 ½ to 4 cups all-purpose flour
⅓ cup granulated sugar
1 teaspoon salt
2 packages regular or quick-acting active
*   dry yeast*
1 cup very warm milk (120° to 130°)
⅓ cup margarine or butter, softened
1 egg
1 cup packed brown sugar
½ cup (1 stick) margarine or butter
¼ cup dark corn syrup
¾ cup pecan halves
2 tablespoons margarine or butter,
*   softened*
½ cup chopped pecans
2 tablespoons granulated sugar
2 tablespoons packed brown sugar
1 teaspoon ground cinnamon

Mix 2 cups of the flour, ⅓ cup granulated sugar, the salt and yeast in large bowl. Add milk, ⅓ cup margarine and the egg. Beat on low speed 1 minute, scraping bowl frequently. Beat on medium speed 1 minute, scraping bowl frequently. Stir in enough remaining flour, 1 cup at a time, to make dough easy to handle.

Turn dough onto lightly floured surface; gently roll in flour to coat. Knead about 5 minutes or until smooth and elastic. Place in greased bowl; turn greased side up. Cover and let rise in warm place about 1½ hours or until double. (Dough is ready if indentation remains when touched.)

Grease rectangular pan, 13 × 9 × 2 inches. Heat 1 cup brown sugar and ½ cup margarine to boiling in 1-quart saucepan, stirring constantly; remove from heat. Stir in corn syrup; cool 5 minutes. Pour into pan. Sprinkle with pecan halves.

Punch down dough. Flatten with hands or rolling pin into rectangle, 15 × 10 inches. Spread with 2 tablespoons margarine. Mix remaining ingredients; sprinkle evenly over rectangle. Roll up tightly, beginning at 15-inch side. Pinch edge of dough into roll to seal. Stretch and shape to make even. Cut roll into fifteen 1-inch slices. Place slightly apart in pan. STOP HERE—see **To Store** and **To Cook**.

To serve now, let rise uncovered in warm place about 30 minutes or until double. Heat oven to 350°. Bake 30 to 35 minutes or until golden brown. Invert immediately onto heatproof serving plate or tray. Let pan remain about 1 minute so caramel can drizzle over rolls. *15 rolls.*

Per Roll: Calories 390; Protein 5 g; Carbohydrate 52 g (Dietary Fiber 2 g); Fat 19 g (Unsaturated 16 g, Saturated 3 g); Cholesterol 15 mg; Sodium 300 mg. Percent of U.S. RDA: Vitamin A 16%; Vitamin C *; Calcium 4%; Iron 12%.

To Store

Refrigerator: Cover unbaked rolls tightly and refrigerate at least 12 hours but no longer than 48 hours.

To Cook from Refrigerator

Oven: About 45 minutes before serving, heat oven to 350°. Uncover and bake 30 to 35 minutes or until golden brown. Invert immediately onto heatproof serving plate or tray. Let pan remain about 1 minute so caramel can drizzle over rolls.

Brunch Bread Pudding

If you'd like to make 8 to 10 servings, double all the ingredients in the recipe, except for the French bread. Bake in a 13 × 9 × 2-inch greased rectangular pan.

½ loaf (1-pound size) French bread, torn
*   into 1-inch pieces (about 8 cups)*
2 tablespoons raisins
3 eggs
⅓ cup granulated sugar
½ teaspoon ground cinnamon
Dash of salt
1½ cups milk
2 tablespoons packed brown sugar

Grease square pan, 9 × 9 × 2 inches. Spread bread evenly in pan; sprinkle with raisins. Beat eggs, granulated sugar, cinnamon and salt in medium bowl. Stir in milk; pour over bread. Sprinkle with brown sugar. STOP HERE—see **To Store** and **To Cook.**

To serve now, heat oven to 325°. Bake 50 to 55 minutes or until golden brown. Serve warm. *6 servings.*

Per Serving: Calories 235; Protein 8 g; Carbohydrate 43 g (Dietary Fiber 1 g); Fat 4 g (Unsaturated 2 g, Saturated 2 g); Cholesterol 110 mg; Sodium 330 mg. Percent of U.S. RDA: Vitamin A 6%; Vitamin C *; Calcium 12%; Iron 10%.

To Store

Refrigerator: Cover unbaked casserole tightly and refrigerate no longer than 24 hours.

To Cook from Refrigerator

Oven: About 1¼ hours before serving, heat oven to 325°. Uncover and bake about 1 hour or until golden brown. Serve warm.

Mixed Fruit Bread

This lovely fruit-filled bread is wonderful served with honey butter or soft-style cream cheese with pineapple.

½ cup apple juice
1 cup diced dried fruit and raisin mixture
¾ cup sugar
3 tablespoons vegetable oil
1 teaspoon vanilla
2 eggs
1 cup all-purpose flour
½ cup whole wheat flour
1¼ teaspoons baking powder
½ teaspoon apple pie spice
¼ teaspoon baking soda
¼ teaspoon salt
½ cup coconut, toasted

Heat oven to 350°. Grease bottom only of loaf pan, 8½ × 4½ × 2½ inches. Heat apple juice to boiling in 1-quart saucepan; remove from heat. Stir in dried fruit. Let stand 5 minutes. Mix fruit mixture, sugar, oil, vanilla and eggs in large bowl. Stir in remaining ingredients except coconut. Fold in coconut. Pour into pan.

Bake 45 to 50 minutes or until toothpick inserted in center comes out clean. Cool 10 minutes. Loosen sides of loaf from pan; remove from pan. Cool completely on wire rack. See **To Store** and **To Serve.**

Can be served now. Slice with sharp knife. *1 loaf, 16 slices.*

Per Slice: Calories 140; Protein 2 g; Carbohydrate 26 g (Dietary Fiber 2 g); Fat 4 g (Unsaturated 3 g, Saturated 1 g); Cholesterol 25 mg; Sodium 90 mg. Percent of U.S. RDA: Vitamin A 2%; Vitamin C *; Calcium 2%; Iron 4%.

TO STORE

Refrigerator: Wrap cooled loaf tightly and refrigerate no longer than 10 days.

Freezer: Wrap cooled loaf tightly and label. Freeze no longer than 2 months.

TO SERVE FROM REFRIGERATOR

Slice with a sharp knife.

TO SERVE FROM THE FREEZER

About 30 minutes before serving, unwrap loaf and let stand at room temperature to thaw. Slice with sharp knife.

Three-Fruit Medley

This luscious fruit mix is wonderful topped with sherbet or frozen yogurt. It's also delicious served over angel food or pound cake slices.

> *2 cups pineapple juice**
> *½ cup dry white wine or apple juice*
> *¼ teaspoon ground mace*
> *2 three-inch sticks cinnamon*
> *2 cups cubed fresh pineapple or 1 can (20 ounces) pineapple chunks in juice, drained**
> *4 oranges, peeled and sectioned*

To Complete Recipe:
> *1 can (16 ounces) pitted dark sweet cherries, chilled and drained*

Heat pineapple juice, wine, mace and cinnamon to boiling in 2-quart saucepan; reduce heat.

Cover and simmer 5 minutes; remove from heat. Stir in pineapple and oranges. Pour into glass or plastic bowl. See **TO STORE** and **TO SERVE**. *8 servings, about ⅔ cup each.*

Microwave: Mix pineapple juice, wine, mace and cinnamon in 1½-quart microwavable casserole. Cover and microwave on Medium (50%) about 6 minutes or until boiling. Stir in pineapple and oranges.

*If using canned pineapple, reserve juice drained from pineapple, then add enough pineapple juice to measure 2 cups.

Per Serving: Calories 125; Protein 1 g; Carbohydrate 33 g (Dietary Fiber 3 g); Fat 0 g (Unsaturated 0 g, Saturated 0 g); Cholesterol 0 mg; Sodium 5 mg. Percent of U.S. RDA: Vitamin A 2%; Vitamin C 50%; Calcium 4%; Iron 4%.

TO STORE

Refrigerator: Refrigerate tightly covered at least 4 hours but no longer than 48 hours.

TO SERVE FROM REFRIGERATOR

Drain fruit, reserving juice. Stir cherries into fruit. Serve fruit with some of the juice if desired.

2
Jump-Start Weeknight Mainstays

Chicken-Asparagus Pot Pies (page 61)

Mexicali Steak

2 tablespoons all-purpose flour
½ teaspoon ground cumin
1 pound beef boneless round, tip or
    chuck steak, about ¾ inch thick
1 tablespoon vegetable oil
2 cans (10 ounces each) diced tomatoes
    with chili peppers, undrained
¼ cup beef broth
1 tablespoon chopped fresh or 1 teaspoon
    dried cilantro leaves
⅛ teaspoon red pepper sauce
1 large onion, sliced
2 medium carrots, sliced (about 1 cup) or
    8 baby carrots cut lengthwise in half

To Complete Recipe:
    4 cups hot cooked rice or pasta

Mix flour and cumin. Sprinkle 1 side of beef steak with half of the flour mixture; pound in. Turn beef; pound in remaining flour mixture. Cut beef into 4 pieces.

Heat oil in 10-inch skillet over medium heat until hot. Cook beef in oil about 15 minutes, turning once, until brown. Stir in tomatoes, broth, cilantro and pepper sauce. Heat to boiling; reduce heat. Cover and simmer 40 minutes. Stir in onion and carrots. Heat to boiling; reduce heat. Cover and simmer about 20 minutes or until vegetables are tender. STOP HERE—see **To Store** and **To Reheat.**

To serve now, serve with rice. *4 servings.*

Per Serving: Calories 270; Protein 27 g; Carbohydrate 16 g
(Dietary Fiber 3 g); Fat 12 g (Unsaturated 8 g, Saturated
4 g); Cholesterol 65 mg; Sodium 350 mg. Percent of U.S.
RDA: Vitamin A 90%; Vitamin C 20%; Calcium 6%; Iron
20%.

To Store

Refrigerator: Refrigerate cooked beef mixture tightly covered no longer than 48 hours.

Freezer: Place cooked beef mixture in rectangular baking dish, 11 × 7 × 1½ inches. (If planning to microwave, use microwavable dish.) Refrigerate uncovered 30 minutes. Wrap tightly with aluminum foil and label. Freeze no longer than 2 months.

To Reheat from Refrigerator:

Oven: About 1 hour before serving, heat oven to 350°. Place beef mixture in rectangular baking dish, 11 × 7 × 1½ inches. Cover with aluminum foil and bake 45 to 50 minutes or until hot. Serve with rice.

Microwave: About 25 minutes before serving, place refrigerated beef mixture in rectangular microwavable dish, 11 × 7 × 1½ inches. Cover with plastic wrap, folding back 1 corner to vent. Microwave on Medium (50%) about 20 minutes, rotating dish ½ turn after 10 minutes, until hot. Serve with rice.

To Reheat from Freezer

Oven: About 1¼ hours before serving, heat oven to 350°. Bake in covered dish about 1 hour or until hot. Serve with rice.

Microwave: About 35 minutes before serving, cover frozen beef mixture loosely with waxed paper and microwave on Medium (50%) 25 to 30 minutes, rotating dish ½ turn after 15 minutes, until hot. Serve with rice.

Mexicali Steak

Robust London Broil

You'll find this steak well worth the marinating time! For a delicious meal, try serving the steak with sautéed onions and mushrooms and steamed asparagus.

> 1 pound high-quality beef flank steak, 1 inch thick
> ½ cup dry white wine or beef broth
> ¼ cup soy sauce
> ¼ cup water
> 1 tablespoon molasses
> ½ teaspoon five-spice powder
> 2 cloves garlic, finely chopped

Cut both sides of beef steak in diamond pattern ⅛ inch deep. Place beef in shallow baking dish. Mix remaining ingredients; pour over beef. See **TO STORE** and **TO COOK**. *4 servings.*

Per Serving: Calories 215; Protein 23 g; Carbohydrate 2 g (Dietary Fiber 0 g); Fat 13 g (Unsaturated 8 g, Saturated 5 g); Cholesterol 70 mg; Sodium 230 mg. Percent of U.S. RDA: Vitamin A *; Vitamin C *; Calcium *; Iron 14%.

TO STORE

Refrigerator: Cover tightly and refrigerate at least 6 hours but no longer than 24 hours, turning beef occasionally.

TO COOK FROM REFRIGERATOR

Broiler: About 15 minutes before serving, set oven control to broil. Remove beef from marinade; discard marinade. Place beef on rack in broiler pan. Broil with top 2 to 3 inches from heat about 5 minutes or until brown; turn. Broil about 5 minutes longer for medium (160°). Cut beef across grain at slanted angle into thin slices.

Design-your-own Pizza

Prebaking the pizza crusts gives you a crisper crust than when you bake them with the toppings. Depending on the size of your oven, you may have to bake the pizzas one at a time.

> Pizza Dough (right)
> 1 pound ground beef, pork, lamb or turkey
> 1 large onion or 1 medium green bell pepper, chopped (about 1 cup)
> 1 teaspoon Italian seasoning
> 2 cloves garlic, finely chopped
> 1 can (8 ounces) pizza sauce
> 1 can (4 ounces) sliced mushrooms or chopped green chilis, drained
> 2 cups shredded mozzarella, Cheddar, Monterey Jack or brick cheese (8 ounces)
> ¼ cup grated Parmesan or Romano cheese

Prepare Pizza Dough. While crusts are baking, cook ground beef, onion, Italian seasoning and garlic in 10-inch skillet over medium heat, stirring occasionally, until beef is brown and onion is tender; drain. Spread pizza sauce over crusts. Sprinkle with beef mixture, mushrooms and cheeses. STOP HERE—see **TO STORE** and **TO COOK**.

To serve now, heat oven. Bake thin-crust pizzas at 425° about 10 minutes, or thick-crust pizzas at 375° about 20 minutes, until cheese is melted and pizzas are bubbly. *2 pizzas, 8 servings each.*

PIZZA DOUGH

*1 package regular or quick-acting active
  dry yeast*
1 cup warm water (105° to 115°)
1½ cups all-purpose flour
1 cup whole wheat flour
2 tablespoons olive or vegetable oil
½ teaspoon salt
Olive or vegetable oil
Cornmeal

Dissolve yeast in warm water in medium bowl. Stir in flours, 2 tablespoons oil and the salt. Beat vigorously 20 strokes. Cover and let rest 20 minutes. Follow directions below for thin or thick crusts.

For thin crusts: Move oven rack to lowest position. Heat oven to 425°. Grease 2 cookie sheets or 12-inch pizza pans with oil. Sprinkle with cornmeal. Divide dough in half; pat each half into 11-inch circle on cookie sheet with floured fingers. Prick dough thoroughly with fork. Bake uncovered about 10 minutes or until crust just begins to brown.

For thick crusts: Move oven rack to lowest position. Heat oven to 375°. Grease 2 square pans, 8 × 8 × 2 inches, with oil. Sprinkle with cornmeal. Divide dough in half; pat each half onto bottom of pan. Cover and let rise in warm place 30 to 45 minutes or until almost double. Bake uncovered 20 to 22 minutes or until crust just begins to brown.

Per Serving: Calories 410; Protein 24 g; Carbohydrate 37 g (Dietary Fiber 4 g); Fat 20 g (Unsaturated 12 g, Saturated 8 g); Cholesterol 50 mg; Sodium 540 mg. Percent of U.S. RDA: Vitamin A 6%; Vitamin C *; Calcium 26%; Iron 18%.

TO STORE

Refrigerator: Cover unbaked pizzas tightly and refrigerate no longer than 48 hours.

Freezer: Wrap unbaked pizzas tightly and label. Freeze no longer than 2 months.

TO COOK FROM REFRIGERATOR

Oven: About 20 to 30 minutes before serving, move oven rack to lowest position and heat oven to 425° for thin-crust pizzas or 375° for thick-crust pizzas. Bake thin-crust pizzas uncovered 10 to 12 minutes, or bake thick-crust pizzas uncovered 20 to 25 minutes, until cheese is melted and pizzas are bubbly.

TO COOK FROM FREEZER

Oven: About 35 minutes to 1¼ hours before serving, heat oven to 375°. Place thin-crust pizzas on 2 greased cookie sheets. Bake thin-crust pizzas uncovered about 25 minutes, or bake thick-crust pizzas uncovered 50 to 60 minutes, until cheese is melted and pizzas are bubbly.

Following page: Design-your-own Pizza (page 38)

Dilled Beef and Bean Soup

You can also use kidney beans or navy beans in this hearty, stick-to-your-ribs soup.

1 tablespoon vegetable oil
1 pound beef boneless round, cut into
1 -inch cubes
3 cups beef broth
1 large onion, chopped (about 1 cup)
2 teaspoons dried dill weed
⅛ teaspoon pepper
1 bay leaf
2 medium stalks celery, sliced (about 1
cup)
2 medium carrots, sliced (about 1 cup)
1 can (15 ounces) black beans, rinsed
and drained

To Complete Recipe:
¼ cup sour cream

Heat oil in Dutch oven over medium heat until hot. Cook beef in oil about 15 minutes, stirring occasionally, until brown; drain. Stir in broth, onion, dill weed, pepper and bay leaf. Heat to boiling; reduce heat. Cover and simmer 30 to 45 minutes or until beef is almost tender.

Stir in celery and carrots. Heat to boiling; reduce heat. Cover and simmer about 15 minutes or until vegetables are tender. Remove bay leaf. Stir in beans. STOP HERE—see **To Store** and **To Reheat.**

To complete recipe and serve now, heat until hot. Top each serving with sour cream. *4 servings, about 1⅓ cups each.*

Per Serving: Calories 350; Protein 33 g; Carbohydrate 33 g (Dietary Fiber 8 g); Fat 13 g (Unsaturated 8 g, Saturated 5 g); Cholesterol 60 mg; Sodium 770 mg. Percent of U.S. RDA:Vitamin A 98%; Vitamin C *; Calcium 12%; Iron 26%.

To Store

Refrigerator: Refrigerate soup tightly covered no longer than 48 hours.

Freezer: Cool soup 30 minutes. Place in labeled airtight 2-quart freezer container. Freeze no longer than 2 months.

To Reheat from Refrigerator

Stove Top: About 25 minutes before serving, heat soup in 3-quart saucepan over medium heat, stirring occasionally, until hot. Top each serving with sour cream.

Microwave: About 15 minutes before serving, place refrigerated soup in 2-quart microwavable casserole. Cover and microwave on High 10 to 12 minutes, stirring after 5 minutes until hot. Top each serving with sour cream.

To Reheat from Freezer

Stovetop: About 40 minutes before serving, dip container into hot water to loosen; remove container. Cover and heat in 3-quart saucepan over medium heat, turning and stirring occasionally, until hot. Top each serving with sour cream.

Microwave: About 35 minutes before serving, remove lid from freezer container; place container upside down in 2-quart microwavable casserole. Microwave on High 5 minutes; remove container. Cover and microwave on High 10 to 15 minutes longer, breaking up and stirring every 5 minutes until hot. Top each serving with sour cream.

Orange-glazed Meat Loaves

1 pound ground pork or beef
½ teaspoon grated orange peel
½ cup orange juice
½ cup quick-cooking oats
1 tablespoon chopped fresh or 1 teaspoon freeze-dried chives
1 teaspoon ground mustard
½ teaspoon salt
⅛ teaspoon pepper
1 egg

To Complete Recipe:
Orange Glaze (right)

Mix all ingredients except Orange Glaze. Shape mixture into 4 oval loaves, about 4½ × 2½ inches. Place in ungreased square pan, 8 × 8 × 2 inches. (If planning to microwave, place in circle in microwavable pie plate, 9 × 1¼ inches.) STOP HERE—see **To Store** and **To Cook.**

To complete recipe and serve now, prepare Orange Glaze. Heat oven to 350°. Bake uncovered 35 minutes. Brush half of the glaze over loaves. Bake uncovered about 10 minutes longer, brushing once with remaining glaze, until well done (170°). *4 servings.*

Microwave: Prepare Orange Glaze. Cover with waxed paper and microwave on High 7 minutes. Brush half of the glaze over loaves; rotate plate ½ turn. Re-cover and microwave 6 to 8 minutes longer, rotating plate ¼ turn and brushing with remaining glaze after 3 minutes, until well done (170°). Let stand on flat, heatproof surface (not wire rack) 5 minutes.

ORANGE GLAZE

3 tablespoons packed brown sugar
2 teaspoons orange juice
½ teaspoon ground mustard

Mix all ingredients.

Per Serving: Calories 390; Protein 24 g; Carbohydrate 21 g (Dietary Fiber 1 g); Fat 24 g (Unsaturated 16 g, Saturated 8 g); Cholesterol 125 mg; Sodium 330 mg. Percent of U.S. RDA: Vitamin A 2%; Vitamin C 10%; Calcium 2%; Iron 8%.

TO STORE

Refrigerator: Cover unbaked meat loaves tightly and refrigerate no longer than 48 hours.

Freezer: Wrap unbaked meat loaves tightly and label. Freeze no longer than 2 months.

TO COOK FROM REFRIGERATOR

Oven: About 1¼ hours before serving, prepare Orange Glaze. Heat oven to 350°. Uncover and bake 50 minutes. Brush half of the glaze over loaves. Bake uncovered about 10 minutes longer, brushing once with remaining glaze, until well done (170°).

Microwave: About 20 minutes before serving, prepare Orange Glaze. Cover refrigerated loaves with waxed paper and microwave on High 11 minutes. Brush half of the glaze over loaves; rotate plate ¼ turn. Re-cover and microwave 5 to 7 minutes longer, rotating plate ¼ turn and brushing with remaining glaze after 3 minutes, until well done (170°). Let stand on flat, heat-proof surface (not wire rack) 5 minutes.

To Cook from Freezer

Oven: About 1¼ hours before serving, prepare Orange Glaze. Heat oven to 350°. Uncover and bake 50 minutes. Brush half of the glaze over loaves. Bake uncovered about 10 minutes longer, brushing once with remaining glaze, until well done (170°).

Microwave: For frozen loaves, follow directions for microwaving refrigerated loaves.

Mushroom-Cheese Burgers

Use your favorite cheese in the filling of these juicy burgers.

> *1 teaspoon margarine or butter*
> *½ cup chopped mushrooms*
> *1 small onion, chopped (about ¼ cup)*
> *2 tablespoons shredded Cheddar cheese*
> *1 tablespoon grated Parmesan cheese*
> *1 pound ground beef*

Heat margarine in 8-inch skillet until melted. Cook mushrooms and onion in margarine over medium heat, stirring frequently, until mushrooms and onion are tender; remove from heat. Mix mushroom mixture and cheeses. Shape ground beef into 8 thin patties, 4 inches in diameter. Place one-fourth of the mushroom mixture on center of each of 4 patties to within ¼ inch of edge. Top with remaining patties; press edges to seal. STOP HERE—see **To Store** and **To Cook.**

To serve now, set oven control to broil. Place patties on rack in broiler pan. Broil with tops about 4 inches from heat 10 to 14 minutes for medium doneness (160°), turning once. *4 servings.*

Grill: Grill patties uncovered about 4 inches from medium coals 14 to 16 minutes, turning once, until at least medium doneness (160°) in center.

Per Serving: Calories 270; Protein 20 g; Carbohydrate 3 g (Dietary Fiber 1 g); Fat 20 g (Unsaturated 12 g, Saturated 8 g); Cholesterol 75 mg; Sodium 120 mg. Percent of U.S. RDA: Vitamin A 2%; Vitamin C *; Calcium 4%; Iron 12%.

To Store

Freezer: Place uncooked patties on cookie sheet. Freeze uncovered about 1 hour or until firm. Place patties in labeled airtight freezer container. Freeze no longer than 2 months.

To Cook from Freezer

Broiler: About 20 minutes before serving, set oven control to broil. Place frozen patties on rack in broiler pan. Broil with tops about 4 inches from heat 11 to 12 minutes, turning once, until at least medium doneness (160°) in center.

Grill: About 20 minutes before serving, grill frozen patties about 4 inches from medium coals 19 to 20 minutes, turning after 11 minutes, until at least medium doneness (160°) in center.

Hungarian Goulash

1 tablespoon vegetable oil or bacon fat
1½ pounds beef boneless chuck, tip or
*   round roast or pork boneless shoulder,*
*   cut into ¾-inch cubes*
1 cup beef broth
3 tablespoons paprika
1½ teaspoons salt
½ teaspoon caraway seed
¼ teaspoon pepper
3 large onions, chopped (about 3 cups)
2 cloves garlic, chopped
1 can (8 ounces) whole tomatoes,
*   undrained*
¼ cup cold water
2 tablespoons all-purpose flour

To Complete Recipe:
    6 cups hot cooked noodles

Heat oil in Dutch oven or 12-inch skillet until hot. Cook beef in oil about 15 minutes, stirring occasionally, until brown; drain. Stir in remaining ingredients except water, flour and noodles; break up tomatoes. Heat to boiling; reduce heat. Cover and simmer about 1¼ hours, stirring occasionally, until beef is tender. Shake water and flour in tightly covered container; slowly stir into beef mixture. Heat to boiling, stirring constantly. Boil and stir 1 minute. STOP HERE—see **To Store** and **To Reheat.**

To serve now, serve over noodles. *6 servings, about 2 cups each.*

Per Serving: Calories 650; Protein 37 g; Carbohydrate 52 g (Dietary Fiber 5 g); Fat 35 g (Unsaturated 22 g, Saturated 13 g); Cholesterol 150 mg; Sodium 1040 mg. Percent of U.S. RDA: Vitamin A 22%; Vitamin C 6%; Calcium 6%; Iron 36%.

To Store

Refrigerator: Cover goulash tightly and refrigerate no longer than 4 days.

Freezer: Place goulash in labeled airtight 1½-quart freezer container. Freeze no longer than 2 months.

To Reheat from Refrigerator

Stovetop: About 20 minutes before serving, cover and heat in 3-quart saucepan over medium heat about 15 minutes, stirring occasionally, until hot and bubbly. Serve over noodles.

Microwave: About 15 minutes before serving, place refrigerated goulash in 2-quart microwavable casserole. Cover tightly and microwave on High 13 to 15 minutes, stirring every 5 minutes, until hot and bubbly. Serve over noodles.

To Reheat from Freezer

Stovetop: About 45 minutes before serving, dip container into hot water to loosen; remove container. Cover tightly and heat goulash and ¼ cup water in 3-quart saucepan over medium-low heat about 30 minutes, turning and stirring occasionally, until hot and bubbly. Serve over noodles.

Microwave: About 20 minutes before serving, remove lid from freezer container; place container upside down in 2-quart microwavable casserole. Microwave on High 5 minutes; remove container. Cover and microwave 10 to 15 minutes longer, breaking up and stirring every 5 minutes, until hot and bubbly. Serve over noodles.

Saucy Meatballs

3 pounds ground beef
1½ cups dry bread crumbs
¾ cup milk
2 teaspoons salt
1½ teaspoons Worcestershire sauce
¼ teaspoon pepper
1 medium onion, finely chopped (about ½
*   cup)*
3 eggs

To Complete Recipe:
  For each meal, 1 jar (about 24 ounces)
   spaghetti sauce or Alfredo, sweet-and-
   sour or stroganoff simmer sauce
   (about 3 cups)
  For each meal, 6 cups hot cooked
   spaghetti or rice, if desired

Heat oven to 400°. Mix all ingredients except spaghetti sauce and spaghetti. Shape one-third of mixture at a time by level tablespoonfuls into 1-inch balls. Place in ungreased jelly roll pan, 15½ × 10½ × 1 inch. Bake uncovered about 15 minutes or until no longer pink in center. STOP HERE—see **To Store** and **To Reheat.**

To complete recipe and serve now, mix 24 meatballs and the spaghetti sauce in 3-quart saucepan. Heat to boiling; reduce heat. Cover and simmer about 15 minutes, stirring occasionally, until hot. Serve over spaghetti. *Enough for 4 meals—6 servings of 4 meatballs each (about 8 dozen meatballs).*

Microwave: Mix 24 meatballs and the spaghetti sauce in 2-quart microwavable casserole. Cover and microwave on High 8 to 10 minutes, stirring after 5 minutes, until hot. Serve over spaghetti.

To Store

Refrigerator: Refrigerate tightly covered no longer than 4 days.

Freezer: Cool meatballs 5 minutes. Freeze uncovered 15 minutes. Place meatballs in airtight freezer container; repeat with remaining meatballs. Freeze no longer than 2 months.

To Reheat from Refrigerator

Stovetop: About 15 minutes before serving, heat 24 meatballs and the spaghetti sauce to boiling in 3-quart saucepan; reduce heat. Cover and simmer about 15 minutes, stirring occasionally, until hot. Serve over spaghetti.

Microwave: About 15 minutes before serving, mix 24 refrigerated meatballs and the spaghetti sauce in 2-quart microwavable casserole. Cover and microwave on High 10 to 12 minutes, stirring after 5 minutes, until hot. Serve over spaghetti.

To Reheat from Freezer

Stovetop: About 30 minutes before serving, heat 24 meatballs and the spaghetti sauce to boiling in 3-quart saucepan; reduce heat. Cover and simmer about 25 minutes, stirring occasionally, until hot. Serve over spaghetti.

Microwave: About 25 minutes before serving, mix 24 frozen meatballs and the spaghetti sauce in 2-quart microwavable casserole. Cover and microwave on High 15 to 20 minutes, stirring every 5 minutes, until hot. Serve over spaghetti.

Per Serving: Calories 170; Protein 11 g; Carbohydrate 8 g (Dietary Fiber 1 g); Fat 11 g (Unsaturated 7 g, Saturated 4 g); Cholesterol 60 mg; Sodium 460 mg. Percent of U.S. RDA: Vitamin A 2%; Vitamin C *; Calcium 4%; Iron 8%.

Easy Lasagne

This lasagne is perfect for freezing! Placing the mozzarella under the spaghetti sauce keeps it softer than if it were sprinkled over the top. If you want to keep your baking pan free for other uses, line it with aluminum foil. Once the lasagne is frozen, remove the foil and lasagne from the pan, wrap tightly, and you can use your pan again.

> *2 cups ricotta or small curd creamed cottage cheese*
> *½ cup grated Parmesan cheese*
> *2 tablespoons chopped fresh parsley*
> *1 tablespoon chopped fresh or 1½ teaspoons dried oregano leaves*
> *8 cups (½ recipe) Italian Spaghetti Sauce (see page 51)*
> *12 uncooked lasagne noodles*
> *2 cups shredded mozzarella cheese (8 ounces)*
> *¼ cup grated Parmesan cheese*

To Complete Recipe:
> *Shredded mozzarella cheese, if desired*

Mix ricotta cheese, ½ cup Parmesan cheese, the parsley and oregano. Spread 2 cups spaghetti sauce in ungreased rectangular pan, 13 × 9 × 2 inches; top with 4 noodles. Spread cheese mixture over noodles. Spread with 2 cups Italian Spaghetti Sauce and top with 4 noodles; repeat with 2 cups spaghetti sauce and 4 noodles. Sprinkle with 2 cups mozzarella cheese. Spread with remaining spaghetti sauce. Sprinkle with ¼ cup Parmesan cheese. STOP HERE—see **To Store** and **To Cook.**

To complete recipe and serve now, heat oven to 350°. Cover with aluminum foil and bake 30 minutes. Uncover and bake about 30 minutes longer or until hot and bubbly. Sprinkle with mozzarella cheese. Let stand 15 minutes before cutting. *8 servings.*

Per Serving: Calories 755; Protein 47 g; Carbohydrate 47g (Dietary Fiber 4 g); Fat 44 g (Unsaturated 26 g, Saturated 18 g); Cholesterol 130 mg; Sodium 2350 mg. Percent of U.S. RDA: Vitamin A 26%; Vitamin C 32%; Calcium 58%; Iron 30%.

To Store

Refrigerator: Cover unbaked lasagne tightly with aluminum foil and refrigerate no longer than 24 hours.

Freezer: Wrap unbaked lasagne tightly with aluminum foil and label. Freeze no longer than 2 months.

To Cook from Refrigerator

Oven: About 1½ hours before serving, heat oven to 350°. Bake in covered pan 45 minutes. Uncover and bake 15 to 20 minutes longer or until hot and bubbly. Sprinkle with mozzarella cheese. Let stand 15 minutes before cutting.

To Cook from Freezer

Oven: About 2 hours before serving, heat oven to 350°. Bake in covered pan 45 minutes. Uncover and bake 35 to 45 minutes longer or until hot and bubbly. Sprinkle with mozzarella cheese. Let stand 15 minutes before cutting.

Easy Lasagne

Beef-stuffed Peppers

When you freeze these peppers, you'll find they release some water when you bake them. This won't affect their great taste, but you may want to remove them from the baking dish with a slotted spoon.

⅓ cup uncooked rosamarina (orzo) pasta
2 large green or red bell peppers, cut
*   lengthwise in half**
½ pound ground beef
1 medium onion, chopped (about ½ cup)
1 package (3 ounces) cream cheese,
*   softened*
1 medium carrot, shredded (about ⅔ cup)
1 tablespoon chopped fresh or 1 teaspoon
*   dried oregano leaves*
½ teaspoon salt
¼ teaspoon garlic powder
⅛ teaspoon pepper
¼ cup crumbled feta cheese (1 ounce)

Cook pasta as directed on package; drain. Remove seeds and membranes from bell peppers; rinse. Cook peppers in enough boiling water to cover in 3-quart saucepan 2 minutes; drain.

Cook ground beef and onion in 10-inch skillet over medium heat, stirring occasionally, until beef is brown and onion is tender; drain. Stir in cream cheese. Stir in pasta and remaining ingredients except feta cheese. Divide beef mixture among pepper halves. Place pepper halves, cut sides up, in ungreased square baking dish, 8 × 8 × 2 inches. Sprinkle with feta cheese. STOP HERE—See **To Store** and **To Cook**.

To serve now, heat oven to 375°. Cover with aluminum foil and bake about 50 minutes or until hot. *4 servings.*

*If following freezing directions, do not cook bell peppers in boiling water.

Per Serving: Calories 280; Protein 14 g; Carbohydrate 17 g (Dietary Fiber 2 g); Fat 18 g (Unsaturated 9 g, Saturated 9 g); Cholesterol 65 mg; Sodium 490 mg. Percent of U.S. RDA: Vitamin A 50%; Vitamin C 30%; Calcium 8%; Iron 12%.

To Store

Refrigerator: Cover unbaked filled peppers tightly with aluminum foil and refrigerate no longer than 48 hours.

Freezer: Wrap unbaked filled peppers tightly with aluminum foil and label. Freeze no longer than 2 months.

To Cook from Refrigerator

Oven: About 1 hour before serving, heat oven to 375°. Bake in covered dish about 50 minutes or until hot.

To Cook from Freezer

Oven: About 1½ hours before serving, heat oven to 375°. Bake in covered dish 1 hour to 1 hour 10 minutes or until hot.

Spicy Chili

When microwaving frozen chili, sometimes you'll find the lid does not fit. Place it on the casserole as best you can—as the chili thaws and heats, the lid will settle on the edge.

> *2 pounds ground beef*
> *2 large onions, chopped (about 2 cups)*
> *3 cans (28 ounces each) whole tomatoes, undrained*
> *3 cans (15 to 16 ounces each) beans (such as kidney, great northern, black, chili or lima beans), drained*
> *1 can (15 ounces) tomato sauce*
> *1 can (4 ounces) chopped green chilis*
> *¼ cup chili powder*
> *1 tablespoon ground cumin*
> *½ teaspoon salt*
> *½ teaspoon pepper*

To Complete Recipe:
> *Shredded Cheddar cheese, if desired*
> *Chopped green onion, if desired*

Cook ground beef and onions in 6-quart Dutch oven over medium heat about 15 minutes, stirring occasionally, until beef is brown and onion is tender; drain. Stir in remaining ingredients except cheese and green onion; break up tomatoes. Heat to boiling; reduce heat. Simmer uncovered 1¼ hours. Spoon off fat if necessary. STOP HERE—see **To Store** and **To Reheat.**

To complete recipe and serve now, top each serving with cheese and green onion. *Enough for 3 meals of 4 (1½-cup) servings each.*

Per Serving: Calories 295; Protein 22 g; Carbohydrate 33 g (Dietary Fiber 10 g); Fat 13 g (Unsaturated 8 g, Saturated 5 g); Cholesterol 45 mg; Sodium 970 mg. Percent of U.S. RDA: Vitamin A 25%; Vitamin C 36%; Calcium 10%; Iron 32%.

TO STORE

Refrigerator: Refrigerate tightly covered no longer than 4 days.

Freezer: Divide chili among 3 labeled airtight 2-quart freezer containers. Cool quickly (see page 7). Freeze no longer than 2 months.

TO REHEAT FROM REFRIGERATOR

Stovetop: About 15 minutes before serving, cover and heat about 6 cups chili in 2-quart saucepan over medium heat 7 to 9 minutes, stirring occasionally, until hot. Top each serving with cheese and green onion.

Microwave: About 15 minutes before serving, place about 6 cups refrigerated chili in 2-quart microwavable casserole. Cover tightly and microwave on High 10 to 12 minutes, stirring every 4 minutes, until hot. Top each serving with cheese and green onion.

TO REHEAT FROM FREEZER

Stovetop: About 45 minutes before serving, dip 1 container into hot water to loosen; remove container. Cover and heat chili and ½ cup water in 2-quart saucepan over medium-high heat 20 minutes, turning and stirring occasionally. Uncover and heat about 15 minutes longer, stirring occasionally, until hot. Top each serving with cheese and green onion.

Microwave: About 30 minutes before serving, remove lid from 1 freezer container; place container upside down in 2-quart microwavable casserole. Microwave on High 5 minutes; remove container. Cover and microwave 20 to 25 minutes, breaking up and stirring every 5 minutes, until hot. Top each serving with cheese and green onion.

Fiesta Pork Chili

1 large onion, chopped (about 1 cup)
2 medium green bell peppers, chopped
*   (about 2 cups)*
2 cloves garlic, finely chopped
1 pound ground pork
2 cups salsa
2 teaspoons chili powder
2 cans (15 to 16 ounces each) pinto
*   beans, rinsed and drained*
2 cans (16 ounces each) whole tomatoes,
*   undrained*
1 package (16 ounces) frozen corn with
*   red and green peppers*

To Complete Recipe:
*   Sour cream, if desired*

Cook onion, bell peppers, garlic and ground pork in Dutch oven over medium heat, stirring frequently, until pork is no longer pink; drain if necessary. Stir in remaining ingredients, breaking up tomatoes. Heat to boiling; reduce heat. Cover and simmer 30 minutes. STOP HERE—see **To Store** and **To Reheat**.

To complete recipe and serve now, top each serving with sour cream. *6 servings.*

Per Serving: Calories 435; Protein 27 g; Carbohydrate 59 g (Dietary Fiber 13 g); Fat 16 g (Unsaturated 10 g, Saturated 6 g); Cholesterol 45 mg; Sodium 1540 mg. Percent of U.S. RDA: Vitamin A 20%; Vitamin C 30%; Calcium 12%; Iron 30%.

To Store

Refrigerator: Refrigerate tightly covered no longer than 4 days.

Freezer: Cool chili 30 minutes. Place in labeled airtight 2-quart freezer containers. Freeze no longer than 2 months.

To Reheat from Refrigerator

Stovetop: About 15 minutes before serving, cover and heat in 2-quart saucepan over medium heat 7 to 9 minutes, stirring occasionally, until hot. Top each serving with sour cream.

Microwave: About 15 minutes before serving, place chili in 2-quart microwavable casserole. Cover tightly and microwave on High 10 to 12 minutes, stirring every 4 minutes, until hot. Top each serving with sour cream.

To Reheat from Freezer

Stovetop: About 45 minutes before serving, dip container into hot water to loosen; remove container. Cover and heat chili and ½ cup water in 2-quart saucepan over medium-high heat 20 minutes, turning and stirring occasionally. Uncover and heat about 15 minutes longer, stirring occasionally, until hot. Top each serving with sour cream.

Microwave: About 30 minutes before serving, remove lid from freezer container; place container upside down in 2-quart microwavable casserole. Microwave on High 5 minutes; remove container. Cover and microwave 20 to 25 minutes, breaking up and stirring every 5 minutes, until hot. Top each serving with sour cream.

Italian Spaghetti Sauce

*4 pounds bulk Italian sausage or ground
   beef (or 2 pounds of each)*
2 tablespoons olive or vegetable oil
*6 medium onions, finely chopped (about
   3 cups)*
*1 large green bell pepper, finely chopped
   (about 1½ cups)*
12 cloves garlic, finely chopped
*4 cans (16 ounces each) whole tomatoes,
   undrained*
3 cans (15 ounces each) tomato sauce
*¼ cup chopped fresh or 2 tablespoons
   dried oregano leaves*
*¼ cup chopped fresh or 2 tablespoons
   dried basil leaves*
2 tablespoons sugar
2 teaspoons salt
½ teaspoon pepper
1 cup red wine or beef broth

To Complete Recipe:
   Hot cooked pasta, if desired

Cook sausage in 6-quart Dutch oven over medium-high heat about 15 minutes, stirring occasionally, until brown. Remove from Dutch oven and drain.

Heat oil in Dutch oven over medium heat until hot. Cook onions, bell pepper and garlic in oil, stirring occasionally, until onions are tender. Stir in sausage and remaining ingredients except wine, pasta and cheese; break up tomatoes. Heat to boiling, stirring occasionally; reduce heat. Simmer uncovered 2 hours, stirring occasionally. Stir in wine. Simmer uncovered 2 hours longer, stirring occasionally. STOP HERE—see **To Store** and **To Reheat.**

To complete recipe and serve now, serve over pasta. *Enough for 4 meals of 6 (⅔-cup) servings each.*

Per Serving: Calories 460; Protein 25 g; Carbohydrate 20 g (Dietary Fiber 3 g); Fat 31 g (Unsaturated 20 g, Saturated 11 g); Cholesterol 90 mg; Sodium 1980 mg. Percent of U.S. RDA: Vitamin A 16%; Vitamin C 30%; Calcium 10%; Iron 20%.

To Store

Refrigerator: Cover tightly and refrigerate no longer than 4 days.

Freezer: Divide spaghetti sauce among 4 labeled airtight 1-quart freezer containers. Cool quickly (see page 7). Freeze no longer than 2 months.

To Reheat from Refrigerator

Stovetop: About 10 minutes before serving, heat 4 cups spaghetti sauce in 2-quart saucepan over medium heat 6 to 8 minutes, stirring occasionally, until hot. Serve over pasta.

Microwave: About 10 minutes before serving, place 4 cups refrigerated spaghetti sauce in 1½-quart microwavable casserole. Cover tightly and microwave on High 6 to 8 minutes, stirring after 3 minutes, until hot. Serve over pasta.

To Reheat from Freezer

Stovetop: About 45 minutes before serving, dip 1 container into hot water to loosen; remove container. Cover and heat in 3-quart saucepan over medium heat 25 minutes, turning block and stirring occasionally; reduce heat. Uncover and simmer about 10 minutes or until hot. Serve over pasta.

Microwave: About 20 minutes before serving, remove lid from 1 freezer container; place container upside down in 1½-quart casserole. Microwave on High 5 minutes; remove container. Cover and microwave 10 to 15 minutes longer, breaking up and stirring every 5 minutes, until hot. Serve over pasta.

Savory Barbecued Ribs

If your family or friends enjoy loads of sauce with their ribs, make a double batch of the ketchup mixture and serve with the ribs. Just have plenty of napkins handy!

*4 pounds fresh pork spareribs, cut into
    serving pieces
1 teaspoon salt
⅓ cup ketchup
1 tablespoon chopped fresh cilantro or
    1 teaspoon dried coriander leaves
3 tablespoons apple butter
1 tablespoon Worcestershire sauce*

Place pork spareribs in Dutch oven. Add enough water to cover spareribs (about 3 quarts) and the salt. Heat to boiling; reduce heat. Cover and simmer 40 minutes; drain.

Heat oven to 375°. Mix remaining ingredients. Place spareribs, meaty sides up, on rack in shallow roasting pan. Brush with half of the ketchup mixture. Bake uncovered about 45 minutes, brushing with ketchup mixture 3 times, until tender. STOP HERE—see **To Store** and **To Reheat.**

Can be served now. *4 servings.*

Per Serving: Calories 640; Protein 35 g; Carbohydrate 13 g (Dietary Fiber 0 g); Fat 50 g (Unsaturated 29 g, Saturated 21 g); Cholesterol 160 mg; Sodium 940 mg. Percent of U.S. RDA: Vitamin A 6%; Vitamin C 4%; Calcium 2%; Iron 12%.

To Store

Refrigerator: Cool baked spareribs 30 minutes. Grease rectangular baking dish, 13 × 9 × 2 inches. Place spareribs in dish. Cover tightly with aluminum foil and refrigerate no longer than 48 hours.

Freezer: Cool baked spareribs 30 minutes. Grease rectangular baking dish, 13 × 9 × 2 inches. Place spareribs in dish. Wrap tightly with aluminum foil and label. Freeze no longer than 2 months.

To Reheat From Refrigerator

Oven: About 50 minutes before serving, heat oven to 375°. Bake in covered dish about 40 minutes or until hot.

To Reheat From Freezer

Oven: About 1¼ hours before serving, heat oven to 375°. Bake in covered dish 55 to 60 minutes or until hot.

Savory Barbecued Ribs; Crunchy Coleslaw (page 79)

Almond-stuffed Pork Chops

½ cup chicken broth
¼ cup uncooked quick-cooking brown rice
2 tablespoons finely chopped dried apricots
2 tablespoons slivered almonds, toasted and chopped
2 teaspoons chopped fresh or ¾ teaspoon dried marjoram leaves
2 tablespoons chopped fresh parsley
4 pork loin chops, 1 inch thick (about 2 pounds)

To Complete Recipe:
¼ cup apricot preserves

Mix broth, brown rice, apricots, almonds and marjoram in 1½-quart saucepan. Heat to boiling; reduce heat. Cover and simmer about 10 minutes or until rice is tender. Stir in parsley.

Cut a 3-inch pocket in each pork chop, cutting from fat side almost to bone. Spoon about 2 tablespoons rice mixture into each pocket. Secure pockets with toothpicks.

Set oven control to broil. Place pork on rack in broiler pan. Broil with top 5 to 6 inches from heat 10 minutes. Turn pork. Broil 10 to 15 minutes longer for medium doneness (160°). STOP HERE—see **To Store** and **To Reheat.**

To complete recipe and serve now, heat preserves; brush over pork. *4 servings.*

Per Serving: Calories 515; Protein 32 g; Carbohydrate 25 g (Dietary Fiber 2 g); Fat 33 g (Unsaturated 21 g, Saturated 12 g); Cholesterol 100 mg; Sodium 160 mg. Percent of U.S. RDA: Vitamin A 4%; Vitamin C *; Calcium 4%; Iron 12%.

To Store

Refrigerator: Place broiled pork in square baking dish, 8 × 8 × 2 inches. Cover tightly with aluminum foil and refrigerate no longer than 48 hours.

Freezer: Place broiled pork in square baking dish, 8 × 8 × 2 inches. Wrap tightly with aluminum foil and label. Freeze no longer than 2 months.

To Reheat from Refrigerator

Oven: About 50 minutes before serving, heat oven to 375°. Bake in covered dish 35 to 40 minutes or until stuffing is hot in center and meat thermometer in stuffing reads 160°. Heat preserves; brush over pork.

To Reheat from Freezer

Oven: About 1¼ hours before serving, heat oven to 375°. Bake in covered dish about 1 hour or until stuffing is hot in center and meat thermometer in stuffing reads 160°. Heat preserves; brush over pork.

Pork Sloppy Joes

1 pound ground pork or beef
1 large onion, chopped (about 1 cup)
1 small green bell pepper, chopped (about ½ cup)
1 can (14½ ounces) stewed tomatoes with jalapeño chilis and spices, undrained
¼ cup chili sauce
1 tablespoon chopped fresh or 1 teaspoon dried thyme leaves
2 teaspoons prepared mustard
1 teaspoon Worcestershire sauce
¼ teaspoon celery seed
1 tablespoon cold water
1 teaspoon cornstarch

To Complete Recipe:
   6 hamburger buns, split and toasted

Cook ground pork, onion and bell pepper in 10-inch skillet over medium heat about 5 minutes, stirring occasionally, until pork is brown; drain. Stir in tomatoes, chili sauce, thyme, mustard, Worcestershire sauce and celery seed. Heat to boiling; reduce heat. Cover and simmer 5 minutes.

Mix water and cornstarch; stir into pork mixture. Boil and stir 1 minute or until thickened. STOP HERE—see **To Store** and **To Reheat.**

To complete recipe and serve now, spoon onto buns. *6 sandwiches.*

***

Per Sandwich: Calories 375; Protein 19 g; Carbohydrate 37 g (Dietary Fiber 3 g); Fat 18 g (Unsaturated 12 g, Saturated 6 g); Cholesterol 50 mg; Sodium 560 mg. Percent of U.S. RDA: Vitamin A 8%; Vitamin C 20%; Calcium 8%; Iron 14%.

To Store

Refrigerator: Refrigerate pork mixture tightly covered no longer than 48 hours.

Freezer: Cool pork mixture 30 minutes. Place in labeled airtight 1½-quart freezer container. Freeze no longer than 2 months.

To Reheat from Refrigerator

Stovetop: About 15 minutes before serving, cover and heat pork mixture in 3-quart saucepan over medium heat, stirring frequently, until hot and bubbly. Spoon onto buns.

Microwave: About 10 minutes before serving, place refrigerated pork mixture in 1½-quart microwavable casserole. Cover and microwave on High 8 to 10 minutes, stirring every 3 minutes, until hot and bubbly. Spoon onto buns.

To Reheat from Freezer

Stovetop: About 20 minutes before serving, dip container into hot water to loosen; remove container. Cover and heat in 3-quart saucepan over medium heat, turning and stirring occasionally, until hot and bubbly. Spoon onto buns.

Microwave: About 20 minutes before serving, remove lid from freezer container; place container upside down in 2-quart microwavable casserole. Microwave on High 5 minutes; remove container. Cover and microwave 10 to 15 minutes longer, breaking up and stirring every 5 minutes, until hot and bubbly. Spoon onto buns.

Easy Moussaka

1 pound ground lamb
2 cups chopped peeled eggplant (about ½ medium)
1 cup sliced mushrooms (about 3 ounces)
1 clove garlic, finely chopped
1 jar (14 ounces) spaghetti sauce
½ teaspoon ground cinnamon
2 tablespoons margarine or butter
2 tablespoons all-purpose flour
¼ teaspoon salt
⅛ teaspoon pepper
1 cup milk
2 eggs, beaten
¼ cup shredded sapsago or crumbled blue cheese (1 ounce)

Cook lamb, eggplant, mushrooms and garlic in 10-inch skillet over medium heat, stirring occasionally, until lamb is brown and vegetables are tender; drain. Stir in spaghetti sauce and cinnamon. Place lamb mixture in ungreased 1½-quart casserole.

Heat margarine in 1-quart saucepan over medium heat until melted. Stir in flour, salt and pepper. Cook, stirring constantly, until mixture is smooth and bubbly; remove from heat. Stir in milk. Heat to boiling, stirring constantly. Boil and stir 1 minute. Gradually stir at least half of the hot mixture into eggs; stir back into hot mixture in saucepan. Boil and stir 1 minute. Stir in cheese until melted. Carefully spread egg mixture over lamb mixture. STOP HERE—see **To Store** and **To Cook.**

To serve now, heat oven to 350°. Bake uncovered 30 to 35 minutes or until bubbly and top is set in center. *6 servings, about 1 cup each.*

Per Serving: Calories 315; Protein 18 g; Carbohydrate 14 g (Dietary Fiber 3 g); Fat 21 g (Unsaturated 13 g, Saturated 8 g); Cholesterol 125 mg; Sodium 740 mg. Percent of U.S. RDA: Vitamin A 14%; Vitamin C *; Calcium 12%; Iron 14%.

To Store

Refrigerator: Cover unbaked moussaka tightly and refrigerate no longer than 24 hours.

To Cook from Refrigerator

Oven: About 1 hour before serving, heat oven to 350°. Bake in covered casserole 30 minutes. Uncover and bake 20 to 25 minutes longer or until bubbly and top is set in center.

Lamb Cassoulet

½ pound boneless lamb shoulder, cut into ½-inch cubes
½ pound bulk pork sausage
2 medium onions, sliced and separated into rings
1 medium bell pepper, chopped (about 1 cup)
2 cloves garlic, finely chopped
2 tablespoons chopped fresh or 2 teaspoons dried marjoram leaves
¼ teaspoon pepper
1 can (15 to 16 ounces) navy beans, rinsed and drained
1 can (15 to 16 ounces) garbanzo beans, rinsed and drained
1 can (15 to 16 ounces) lima beans, rinsed and drained
1 can (15 ounces) tomato sauce
½ cup beer or chicken broth

Cook lamb, sausage, onions, bell pepper, garlic, marjoram and pepper in 10-inch skillet over medium heat, stirring occasionally, until lamb and sausage are brown; drain. Spoon lamb mixture into ungreased 2-quart casserole. Stir in remaining ingredients. STOP HERE—see **To Store** and **To Cook.**

To serve now, heat oven to 375°. Cover and bake 50 to 60 minutes, stirring occasionally, until lamb is tender. *4 servings, about 1¾ cups each.*

Per Serving: Calories 590; Protein 40 g; Carbohydrate 74 g (Dietary Fiber 18 g); Fat 23 g (Unsaturated 15 g, Saturated 8 g); Cholesterol 75 mg; Sodium 1590 mg. Percent of U.S. RDA: Vitamin A 12%; Vitamin C 20%; Calcium 16%; Iron 52%.

To Store

Refrigerator: Cover unbaked lamb mixture tightly and refrigerate no longer than 48 hours.

To Cook from Refrigerator

Oven: About 1¾ hours before serving, heat oven to 375°. Bake in covered casserole about 1½ hours, stirring occasionally, until lamb is tender.

Seven-Layer Chef's Salad

This salad is also great with cooked chicken substituted for the ham, or try smoked turkey and Swiss cheese.

> *3 cups bite-size pieces lettuce*
> *3 cups bite-site pieces spinach or kale*
> *2 cups chopped fully cooked smoked ham*
> *2 cups cauliflowerets*
> *1 medium zucchini, thinly sliced (about 1 cup)*
> *2 hard-cooked eggs, peeled and sliced*
> *¾ cup mayonnaise or salad dressing*
> *½ cup creamy Italian dressing*
> *1 cup shredded Cheddar cheese (4 ounces)*
> *¼ cup chopped fresh parsley*

Mix lettuce and spinach in large glass bowl. Layer ham and cauliflowerets on lettuce mixture. Place zucchini in center of bowl. Arrange eggs slices around edge of bowl. Mix mayonnaise and Italian dressing; carefully spread over top of salad to edge of bowl. Sprinkle with cheese and parsley. See **To Store** and **To Serve.** *4 servings, about 3 cups each.*

Per Serving: Calories 780; Protein 28 g; Carbohydrate 12 g (Dietary Fiber 3 g); Fat 70 g (Unsaturated 53 g, Saturated 17 g); Cholesterol 210 mg; Sodium 1390 mg. Percent of U.S. RDA: Vitamin A 52%; Vitamin C 100%; Calcium 24%; Iron 20%.

To Store

Refrigerator: Cover tightly and refrigerate no longer than 24 hours.

To Serve from Refrigerator

Toss before serving if desired.

Italian Chicken Rolls

You'll find these rolls equally delicious when you substitute mozzarella cheese for the provolone, and ham for the pastrami.

*4 skinless boneless chicken breast halves
    (about 1 pound)*
*2 slices provolone cheese (2½ ounces),
    cut in half*
4 thin slices pastrami
⅓ cup Italian-style dry bread crumbs
*¼ cup grated Romano or Parmesan
    cheese*
*2 tablespoons finely chopped fresh
    parsley*
¼ cup milk

Grease square pan, 8 × 8 × 2 inches. Flatten each chicken breast half to ¼-inch thickness between plastic wrap or waxed paper. Place 1 piece provolone cheese and 1 slice pastrami on each chicken piece. Fold long sides of each chicken piece over pastrami. Roll up chicken from short side; secure with toothpick.

Mix bread crumbs, cheese and parsley. Dip chicken rolls into milk; coat evenly with bread crumb mixture. Place seam sides down in pan. STOP HERE—see **TO STORE** and **TO COOK.**

To serve now, heat oven to 425°. Bake uncovered about 30 minutes or until juice of chicken is no longer pink when centers of thickest pieces are cut. *4 servings.*

Per Serving: Calories 310; Protein 36 g; Carbohydrate 8 g (Dietary Fiber 0 g); Fat 15 g (Unsaturated 8 g, Saturated 7 g); Cholesterol 100 mg; Sodium 570 mg. Percent of U.S. RDA: Vitamin A 6%; Vitamin C *; Calcium 24%; Iron 10%.

TO STORE

Freezer: Freeze unbaked chicken rolls uncovered about 1 hour or until firm. Wrap tightly and label. Freeze no longer than 2 months.

TO COOK FROM FREEZER

Oven: About 1¼ hours before serving, heat oven to 375°. Bake uncovered about 50 minutes or until juice of chicken is no longer pink when centers of thickest pieces are cut.

Italian Chicken Rolls

Marinated Chicken Kabobs

Serve these zesty kabobs with your favorite pilaf or brown rice.

¼ cup white wine vinegar
¼ cup water
3 tablespoons vegetable oil
2 teaspoons fines herbes
½ teaspoon salt
½ teaspoon Worcestershire sauce
2 cloves garlic, finely chopped
1 pound skinless boneless chicken breast
  halves or thighs, cut into 1½-inch
  pieces
2 small zucchini, cut into ¾-inch slices
½ medium bell pepper, cut into bite-size
  pieces
8 whole medium mushrooms

Mix vinegar, water, oil, fines herbes, salt, Worcestershire sauce and garlic in heavy-duty plastic food-storage bag. Add remaining ingredients to bag. Seal bag and turn to coat. See **To STORE** and **To COOK.** *4 servings.*

Per Serving: Calories 180; Protein 25 g; Carbohydrate 5 g (Dietary Fiber 1 g); Fat 7 g (Unsaturated 5 g, Saturated 2 g); Cholesterol 60 mg; Sodium 130 mg. Percent of U.S. RDA: Vitamin A 2%; Vitamin C 10%; Calcium 2%; Iron 8%.

TO STORE

Refrigerator: Refrigerate at least 4 hours but no longer than 24 hours, turning bag several times.

TO COOK FROM REFRIGERATOR

Broiler: About 15 minutes before serving, set oven control to broil. Grease broiler pan rack. Drain chicken and vegetable pieces. Thread chicken and vegetable pieces on eight 8-inch metal skewers, leaving space between pieces. Place kabobs on rack in broiler pan. Broil with tops about 4 inches from heat about 6 minutes or until brown. Turn kabobs. Broil 4 to 5 minutes longer or until chicken is no longer pink in center.

Chicken-Asparagus Pot Pies

2 tablespoons margarine or butter
2 tablespoons all-purpose flour
1 teaspoon onion powder
¾ teaspoon ground sage
¼ teaspoon salt
⅛ teaspoon pepper
1¼ cups milk
1 package (3 ounces) cream cheese,
  softened
1½ cups ½-inch pieces cooked chicken or
  turkey
1 package (10 ounces) frozen asparagus
  cuts, thawed
1 small carrot, shredded (about ½ cup)
Pastry (right)

Heat margarine in 2-quart saucepan over medium heat until melted. Stir in flour, onion powder, sage, salt and pepper. Cook, stirring constantly, until mixture is smooth and bubbly; remove from heat. Stir in milk. Heat to boiling, stirring constantly. Boil and stir 1 minute. Stir in cream cheese until melted. Stir in chicken, asparagus and carrot; remove from heat.

Heat oven to 425°. Prepare Pastry. Roll pastry into 11-inch square. Cut out four 5-inch circles. Spoon chicken mixture into 4 ungreased 10-ounce custard cups or 8-ounce soufflé dishes. Place pastry circle on top of each custard cup. Turn edges under and flute or press firmly around with tines of fork. Cut slits in pastry to let steam escape. Bake 25 to 30 minutes or until pastry is golden. STOP HERE—see **To Store** and **To Reheat.**

To serve now, let stand 10 minutes. *4 servings.*

Pastry

3 tablespoons shortening
½ cup all-purpose flour
⅛ teaspoon salt
1 to 2 tablespoons cold water

Cut shortening into flour and salt with pastry blender in small bowl until particles are the size of small peas. Sprinkle in water, 1 teaspoon at a time, tossing with fork until all flour is moistened and pastry almost cleans side of bowl. Gather pastry into a ball. Shape into flattened round on lightly floured cloth-covered surface.

> **Per Serving:** Calories 430; Protein 23 g; Carbohydrate 24 g (Dietary Fiber 2 g); Fat 28 g (Unsaturated 18 g, Saturated 10 g); Cholesterol 75 mg; Sodium 420 mg. Percent of U.S. RDA: Vitamin A 54%; Vitamin C 10%; Calcium 14%; Iron 14%.

To Store

Refrigerator: Cool pot pies on wire rack 30 minutes. Cover tightly with aluminum foil and refrigerate no longer than 48 hours.

Freezer: Cool pot pies on wire rack 30 minutes. Wrap tightly with aluminum foil and label. Freeze no longer than 1 month.

To Reheat from Refrigerator

Oven: About 1 hour before serving, heat oven to 375°. Bake in covered custard cups 30 minutes. Uncover and bake about 15 minutes longer or until hot in center. Let stand 10 minutes.

To Reheat from Freezer

Oven: About 1½ hours before serving, heat oven to 375°. Bake in covered custard cups 1 hour. Uncover and bake about 15 minutes longer or until hot in center. Let stand 10 minutes.

Turkey-Chili Enchiladas

You can control the "heat" in these spicy enchiladas by choosing mild, medium or hot green chilies.

> *2 cups chopped cooked turkey or chicken*
> *1 cup shredded Cheddar cheese*
>   *(4 ounces)*
> *1 cup ricotta cheese*
> *1 medium onion, finely chopped (about ½ cup)*
> *1 can (4 ounces) chopped green chilies, drained*
> *¾ teaspoon ground coriander*
> *6 flour tortillas (7 inches in diameter)*
> *1 can (8 ounces) tomato sauce*
> *1 cup salsa*
> *1 tablespoon chopped fresh cilantro, if desired*
> *½ teaspoon chili powder*
> *⅛ teaspoon ground cumin*

To Complete Recipe:
> *½ cup shredded Cheddar cheese (2 ounces)*

Grease rectangular baking dish, 13 × 9 × 2 inches. Mix turkey, 1 cup Cheddar cheese, the ricotta cheese, onion, chilis and coriander. Spoon about ½ cup turkey mixture onto each tortilla; roll tortilla around turkey mixture. Place seam side down in dish. Mix tomato sauce, salsa, chili powder and cumin. STOP HERE— see **TO STORE** and **TO COOK.**

To complete recipe and serve now, heat oven to 350°. Pour tomato sauce mixture over tortillas. Cover with aluminum foil and bake 15 minutes. Sprinkle with ½ cup Cheddar cheese. Bake uncovered about 10 minutes longer or until hot and bubbly. *6 servings.*

Per Serving: Calories 425; Protein 30 g; Carbohydrate 35 g (Dietary Fiber 2 g); Fat 19 g (Unsaturated 9 g, Saturated 10 g); Cholesterol 85 mg; Sodium 1230 mg. Percent of U.S. RDA: Vitamin A 18%; Vitamin C 10%; Calcium 32%; Iron 20%.

TO STORE

Refrigerator: Cover baking dish tightly with aluminum foil, cover tomato sauce mixture tightly and refrigerate no longer than 48 hours.

Freezer: Pour tomato sauce mixture over tortillas. Wrap baking dish tightly with aluminum foil and label. Freeze no longer than 2 months.

TO COOK FROM REFRIGERATOR

Oven: About 1 hour before serving, heat oven to 350°. Pour tomato sauce mixture over tortillas. Re-cover and bake 30 minutes. Sprinkle with ½ cup Cheddar cheese. Bake uncovered about 15 minutes longer or until hot and bubbly.

TO COOK FROM FREEZER

Oven: About 1 hour before serving, heat oven to 375°. Bake in covered pan 45 minutes. Uncover and sprinkle with ½ cup Cheddar cheese. Bake 15 to 20 minutes longer or until hot and bubbly.

Turkey-Chili Enchiladas

Ground Turkey Calzones

Pizza Dough (see page 39)
1 pound ground turkey
1 medium stalk celery, chopped (about ½ cup)
1 medium onion, chopped (about ½ cup)
½ cup spaghetti sauce with mushrooms
2 tablespoons dry bread crumbs
¾ teaspoon fennel seed
½ teaspoon Italian seasoning
1 egg, beaten
2 tablespoons grated Parmesan cheese

To Complete Recipe:
1¼ cups spaghetti sauce with mushrooms

Grease large cookie sheet. Prepare Pizza Dough—except omit second oil ingredient and the cornmeal, and do not bake; cover dough and let rest. Cook turkey, celery and onion in 10-inch skillet over medium heat, stirring occasionally, until turkey is no longer pink and vegetables are tender. Stir in ½ cup spaghetti sauce, the bread crumbs, fennel seed and Italian seasoning; remove from heat.

Heat oven to 350°. Punch down pizza dough. Divide into 6 equal parts. Roll each part into 7-inch circle on lightly floured surface. Spoon ½ cup turkey mixture onto half of each circle. Fold dough carefully over turkey mixture. Lightly moisten edges of dough with water. Pinch edges to seal securely. Cut slits in calzones for steam to escape. Place on cookie sheet.

Brush calzones with egg. Sprinkle with cheese. Bake about 25 minutes or until golden brown. STOP HERE—see **To Store** and **To Reheat.**

To complete recipe and serve now, heat 1¼ cups spaghetti sauce in 1-quart saucepan over medium heat, stirring occasionally, until hot. Serve with calzones. *6 servings.*

Per Serving: Calories 475; Protein 25 g; Carbohydrate 50 g (Dietary Fiber 6 g); Fat 22 g (Unsaturated 17 g, Saturated 5 g); Cholesterol 90 mg; Sodium 770 mg. Percent of U.S. RDA: Vitamin A 8%; Vitamin C *; Calcium 8%; Iron 24%.

To Store

Refrigerator: Cool baked calzones 30 minutes on wire rack. Wrap tightly and refrigerate no longer than 48 hours.

Freezer: Cool baked calzones 30 minutes on wire rack. Wrap tightly and label. Freeze no longer than 2 months.

To Reheat from Refrigerator

Oven: About 30 minutes before serving, heat oven to 350°. Unwrap calzones and place on ungreased cookie sheet. Bake about 20 minutes or until hot. Heat 1¼ cups of spaghetti sauce in 1-quart saucepan over medium heat, stirring occasionally, until hot. Serve with calzones.

To Reheat from Freezer

Oven: About 40 minutes before serving, heat oven to 350°. Unwrap calzones and place on ungreased cookie sheet. Bake 25 to 30 minutes or until hot. Heat 1¼ cups of spaghetti sauce in 1-quart saucepan over medium heat, stirring occasionally, until hot. Serve with calzones.

Dijon Fish with Barley Pilaf

You can substitute imitation bacon bits for the regular bacon, but we don't recommend using nonfat dressing for this recipe.

1 tablespoon margarine or butter
1 medium stalk celery, chopped (about ½ cup)
1 small onion, chopped (about ¼ cup)
2 cups cooked barley
2 medium carrots, shredded (about 1⅓ cups)
¼ cup chopped walnuts
½ teaspoon salt
⅛ teaspoon pepper
4 slices bacon, crisply cooked and crumbled
4 frozen unbreaded fish portions (about 4 ounces each)
¾ cup honey-Dijon or creamy Parmesan dressing

To Complete Recipe:
Chopped fresh parsley, if desired

Heat margarine in 10-inch skillet over medium heat until melted. Cook celery and onion in margarine about 2 minutes, stirring occasionally, until softened; remove from heat. Stir in barley, carrots, walnuts, salt, pepper and bacon. Place about 1 cup barley mixture in each of 4 ungreased 16- to 20-ounce individual casseroles. Top each with frozen fish portion. Pour about 3 tablespoons dressing over each fish portion. STOP HERE—see **To Store** and **To Cook.**

To complete recipe and serve now, heat oven to 400°. Cover each casserole with aluminum foil and bake about 35 minutes or until fish flakes easily with fork. Sprinkle with parsley. *4 servings.*

Per Serving: Calories 520; Protein 29 g; Carbohydrate 34 g (Dietary Fiber 5 g); Fat 32 g (Unsaturated 25 g, Saturated 7 g); Cholesterol 80 mg; Sodium 1000 mg. Percent of U.S. RDA: Vitamin A 100%; Vitamin C 8%; Calcium 10%; Iron 10%.

TO STORE

Refrigerator: Cover each unbaked casserole tightly with aluminum foil and refrigerate no longer than 24 hours.

Freezer: Wrap each casserole tightly with aluminum foil and label. Freeze no longer than 2 months.

TO COOK FROM REFRIGERATOR

Oven: About 40 minutes before serving, heat oven to 400°. Bake in covered casseroles about 30 minutes or until fish flakes easily with fork. Sprinkle with parsley.

TO COOK FROM FREEZER

Oven: About 1 hour before serving, heat oven to 400°. Bake in covered casseroles about 50 minutes or until fish flakes easily with fork. Sprinkle with parsley.

Salmon-Tortellini Salad

Can't find broccoli slaw at the supermarket? Simply substitute coleslaw mix, shredded cabbage or shredded broccoli stems.

Per Serving: Calories 525; Protein 28 g; Carbohydrate 23 g (Dietary Fiber 3 g); Fat 37 g (Unsaturated 30 g, Saturated 7 g); Cholesterol 140 mg; Sodium 730 mg. Percent of U.S. RDA: Vitamin A 72%; Vitamin C 60%; Calcium 18%; Iron 16%.

1 package (7 ounces) dried cheese-filled tricolor or regular tortellini
3 medium carrots, sliced (about 1½ cups)
3 cups broccoli slaw or julienne strips broccoli stems
1 cup sliced mushrooms (about 3 ounces)
¾ cup ranch-style dressing
½ cup mayonnaise or salad dressing
¼ cup milk
1½ tablespoons chopped fresh or 1½ teaspoons dried dill weed
¼ teaspoon lemon pepper
¾ pound cooked salmon or 1 can (14¾ ounces) salmon, drained, flaked and bones removed

To Complete Recipe:
Lettuce leaves

Cook tortellini as directed on package; drain. Rinse in cold water; drain. Mix tortellini and remaining ingredients except salmon and lettuce in large bowl. Fold in salmon. See **TO STORE** and **TO SERVE.** *6 servings, about 2 cups each.*

TO STORE

Refrigerator: Cover tightly and refrigerate at least 4 hours but no longer than 48 hours.

TO SERVE FROM REFRIGERATOR

Stir before serving (stir in small amount of additional milk, if necessary, to make dressing creamy). Serve on lettuce leaves.

Salmon-Tortellini Salad

Cheesy Crab and Broccoli

3 tablespoons margarine or butter
3 tablespoons all-purpose flour
1½ teaspoons chopped fresh or ½
*   teaspoon dried rosemary leaves*
1½ cups milk
½ cup shredded Swiss cheese (2 ounces)
2 tablespoons dry or sweet sherry or 1
*   teaspoon sherry extract*
2 packages (9 or 10 ounces each) frozen
*   broccoli spears or artichoke hearts,*
*   cooked and drained*
8 ounces cooked crabmeat or imitation
*   crabmeat, cut into bite-size pieces*
*   (about 2½ cups)*
½ cup shredded Swiss cheese (2 ounces)

To Complete Recipe:
6 cups hot cooked rice

Heat margarine in 1-quart saucepan over medium heat until melted. Stir in flour and rosemary. Cook, stirring constantly, until mixture is smooth and bubbly; remove from heat. Stir in milk. Heat to boiling, stirring constantly. Boil and stir 1 minute; remove from heat. Stir in ½ cup cheese and the sherry.

Arrange hot broccoli spears in ungreased square baking dish, 8 × 8 × 2 inches. (If planning to microwave, use microwavable dish.) Top with crabmeat. Pour cheese mixture over crabmeat. Sprinkle with ½ cup cheese. STOP HERE—see **To Store** and **To Cook.**

To complete recipe and serve now, heat oven to 350°. Bake uncovered about 20 minutes or until hot. Serve with rice. *6 servings, about 2 cups each.*

Per Serving: Calories 470; Protein 23 g; Carbohydrate 69 g (Dietary Fiber 4 g); Fat 13 g (Unsaturated 8 g, Saturated 5 g); Cholesterol 60 mg; Sodium 1050 mg. Percent of U.S. RDA: Vitamin A 31%; Vitamin C 30%; Calcium 36%; Iron 20%.

To Store

Refrigerator: Cover unbaked mixture tightly and refrigerate no longer than 48 hours.

To Cook from Refrigerator

Oven: About 55 minutes before serving, heat oven to 350°. Uncover and bake uncovered about 45 minutes or until hot. Serve with rice.

Microwave: About 20 minutes before serving, cover refrigerated dish with waxed paper and microwave on Medium (50%) about 18 minutes, rotating dish ½ turn after 9 minutes, until hot. Serve with rice.

Gouda Puffs

3 tablespoons margarine or butter
1 small carrot, shredded (about ½ cup)
1 tablespoon chopped fresh or 1 teaspoon
  freeze-dried chives
¼ cup all-purpose flour
1 tablespoon chopped fresh or 1 teaspoon
  dried thyme leaves
¼ teaspoon garlic powder
1½ cups milk
1½ cups shredded Gouda cheese
  (6 ounces)
4 eggs, separated
½ teaspoon cream of tartar

Grease four 20-ounce casseroles. Heat margarine in 1½-quart saucepan over medium heat until melted. Cook carrot and chives in margarine, stirring frequently, until carrot is tender. Stir in flour, thyme and garlic powder. Cook, stirring constantly, until mixture is smooth and bubbly; remove from heat. Stir in milk. Heat to boiling, stirring constantly. Boil and stir 1 minute. Stir in cheese until melted; remove from heat.

Beat egg yolks in small bowl on high speed until thick and lemon colored. Gradually stir cheese mixture into egg yolks; cool. Beat egg whites and cream of tartar in medium bowl on medium speed until stiff peaks form. Fold egg yolk mixture into egg whites. Spoon into casseroles. STOP HERE—see **To Store** and **To Cook.**

To serve now, heat oven to 350°. Bake uncovered about 30 minutes or until knife inserted halfway between center and edges comes out clean. Serve immediately. *4 servings.*

Per Serving: Calories 380; Protein 21 g; Carbohydrate 14 g (Dietary Fiber 1 g); Fat 27 g (Unsaturated 15 g, Saturated 12 g); Cholesterol 260 mg; Sodium 660 mg. Percent of U.S. RDA: Vitamin A 80%; Vitamin C *; Calcium 46%; Iron 10%.

To Store

Freezer: Wrap unbaked puffs tightly and label. Freeze no longer than 1 month.

To Cook from Freezer

Oven: About 1½ hours before serving, heat oven to 300°. Unwrap puffs and place in shallow pan. Place on oven rack. Fill pan with hot water until ½ inch deep. Bake uncovered 1 hour to 1 hour 10 minutes or until knife inserted halfway between center and edges comes out clean. Serve immediately.

Gruyère Vegetables

This flavorful side dish is especially nice with baked chicken or roast beef.

1 package (16 ounces) frozen mixed
  broccoli, cauliflower and carrots
2 tablespoons margarine or butter
2 tablespoons all-purpose flour
¼ teaspoon salt
¼ teaspoon onion powder
¼ teaspoon caraway seed
1 cup milk
½ cup shredded Gruyère or Swiss cheese
  (2 ounces)
½ cup whole wheat or white soft bread
  crumbs
1 tablespoon margarine or butter, melted

Cook mixed vegetables as directed on package; drain. Heat 2 tablespoons margarine in 1½-quart saucepan over medium heat until melted. Stir in flour, salt, onion powder and caraway seed. Cook, stirring constantly, until mixture is smooth and bubbly; remove from heat. Stir in milk. Heat to boiling, stirring constantly. Boil and stir 1 minute. Stir in cheese until melted. Stir in vegetables.

Place vegetable mixture in ungreased 1½-quart casserole. (If planning to microwave, use microwavable casserole.) Mix bread crumbs and 1 tablespoon margarine. STOP HERE—see **To Store** and **To Cook.**

To serve now, heat oven to 350°. Sprinkle bread crumb mixture around edge of casserole. Bake uncovered about 20 minutes or until crumbs are golden. *4 servings.*

> **Per Serving:** Calories 245; Protein 10 g; Carbohydrate 23 g (Dietary Fiber 3 g); Fat 14 g (Unsaturated 9 g, Saturated 5 g); Cholesterol 20 mg; Sodium 430 mg. Percent of U.S. RDA: Vitamin A 94%; Vitamin C 20%; Calcium 26%; Iron 8%.

To Store

Refrigerator: Cover unbaked casserole tightly, cover bread crumb mixture tightly and refrigerate no longer than 48 hours.

To Cook from Refrigerator

Oven: About 50 minutes before serving, heat oven to 350°. Stir vegetable mixture. Sprinkle bread crumb mixture around edge of casserole. Bake uncovered about 40 minutes or until crumbs are golden and vegetables are hot.

Microwave: About 15 minutes before serving, stir refrigerated vegetable mixture. Sprinkle bread crumb mixture around edge of casserole. Cover loosely with waxed paper and microwave on Medium (50%) 10 to 12 minutes, rotating casserole ¼ turn after 5 minutes, until hot.

Gruyère Vegetables

Three-Cheese Rigatoni

3 cups uncooked rigatoni (about 7
  ounces)
2 medium stalks celery, sliced (about 1
  cup)
1 small carrot, shredded (about ½ cup)
1 container (8 ounces) sour cream–and-
  chives dip
1 cup shredded Colby cheese
  (4 ounces)
1 cup shredded brick cheese
  (4 ounces)
¼ cup grated Parmesan cheese
¼ cup milk
1 tablespoon chopped fresh or 1 teaspoon
  dried basil leaves
¼ cup seasoned dry bread crumbs
1 tablespoon margarine or butter, melted

Cook rigatoni as directed on package; drain. Mix rigatoni and remaining ingredients except bread crumbs and margarine. Place rigatoni mixture in ungreased 2-quart casserole. Mix bread crumbs and margarine. STOP HERE—see **To Store** and **To Cook.**

To serve now, heat oven to 375°. Sprinkle bread crumb mixture around edge of casserole. Bake uncovered 25 to 30 minutes or until hot and bubbly. *6 servings, about 1¾ cups each.*

> **Per Serving:** Calories 515; Protein 22 g; Carbohydrate 58 g (Dietary Fiber 3 g); Fat 23 g (Unsaturated 10 g, Saturated 13 g); Cholesterol 65 mg; Sodium 900 mg. Percent of U.S. RDA: Vitamin A 44%; Vitamin C *; Calcium 36%; Iron 18%.

To Store

Refrigerator: Cover casserole tightly, cover bread crumb mixture tightly and refrigerate no longer than 48 hours.

To Cook from Refrigerator

Oven: About 1 hour before serving, heat oven to 375°. Sprinkle bread crumb mixture around edge of casserole. Bake uncovered about 50 minutes or until hot and bubbly.

Old-fashioned Baked Beans

People have different views as to how thick baked beans should be. If they become too thick, just add a small amount of water until they reach your desired consistency.

10 cups water
2 cups dried navy beans
½ cup packed brown sugar
¼ cup molasses
1 teaspoon salt
6 slices bacon, crisply cooked and
*   crumbled*
1 medium onion, chopped (about ½ cup)
3 cups water

Heat oven to 350°. Heat 10 cups water and the beans to boiling in Dutch oven. Boil uncovered 2 minutes. Stir in remaining ingredients except 3 cups water. Cover and bake 4 hours, stirring occasionally. Stir in 3 cups water. Bake uncovered 2 to 2¼ hours longer, stirring occasionally, until beans are tender and desired consistency. See **TO STORE** and **TO REHEAT**. Can be served now. *10 servings, about ½ cup each.*

Per Serving: Calories 190; Protein 9 g; Carbohydrate 42 g (Dietary Fiber 7 g); Fat 2 g (Unsaturated 1 g, Saturated 1 g); Cholesterol 5 mg; Sodium 280 mg. Percent of U.S. RDA: Vitamin A *; Vitamin C *; Calcium 10%; Iron 16%.

TO STORE

Refrigerator: Cover baked beans tightly and refrigerate no longer than 4 days.

Freezer: Divide baked beans between 2 labeled airtight 3- or 4-cup freezer containers. Cool quickly (see page 7). Freeze no longer than 2 months.

TO REHEAT FROM REFRIGERATOR

Stovetop: About 10 minutes before serving, cover and heat about 2½ cups baked beans in 1-quart saucepan over low heat 5 to 6 minutes, stirring occasionally, until hot.

Microwave: About 5 minutes before serving, place about 2½ cups refrigerated baked beans in 1-quart microwavable casserole. Cover tightly and microwave on High 3 to 4 minutes, stirring after 2 minutes, until hot.

TO REHEAT FROM FREEZER

Stovetop: About 15 minutes before serving, dip 1 container into hot water to loosen; remove container. Cover and heat baked beans and 2 tablespoons water in 1-quart saucepan over low heat 10 to 12 minutes, turning and stirring occasionally, until hot.

Microwave: About 10 minutes before serving, remove lid from 1 freezer container; place container upside down in 1-quart microwavable casserole. Microwave on High 2 minutes; remove container. Cover and microwave 6 to 8 minutes, turning and stirring after 3 minutes, until hot.

Spanish Barley Pilaf

¾ cup sliced mushrooms (about 2 ounces)
⅔ cup uncooked quick-cooking barley
1 cup chicken broth
2 tablespoons chopped green chilis
1 teaspoon chili powder
1 medium onion, chopped (about ½ cup)
1 can (8 ounces) stewed tomatoes,
  undrained

Mix all ingredients in 1½-quart saucepan. Heat to boiling; reduce heat. Cover and simmer about 15 minutes, stirring occasionally, until barley is tender. See **To Store** and **To Reheat.** Can be served now. *4 servings, about ¾ cup each.*

Per Serving: Calories 165; Protein 6 g; Carbohydrate 37 g (Dietary Fiber 6 g); Fat 2 g (Unsaturated 1 g, Saturated 1 g); Cholesterol 0 mg; Sodium 350 mg. Percent of U.S. RDA: Vitamin A 12%; Vitamin C 20%; Calcium 2%; Iron 12%.

To Store

Refrigerator: Cover barley mixture tightly and refrigerate no longer than 48 hours.

Freezer: Place barley mixture in labeled airtight 1½-quart freezer container. Freeze no longer than 2 months.

To Reheat from Refrigerator

Oven: About 50 minutes before serving, heat oven to 375°. Cover and bake in 1½-quart casserole 35 to 40 minutes or until hot.

Microwave: About 10 minutes before serving, place barley mixture in 1½-quart microwavable casserole. Cover and microwave on High 6 to 8 minutes, stirring after 3 minutes, until hot.

To Reheat from Freezer

Oven: About 1½ hours before serving, heat oven to 375°. Dip container into hot water to loosen; remove container. Cover and bake in 1½-quart casserole about 1 hour, turning and stirring occasionally, until hot.

Microwave: About 20 minutes before serving, remove lid from freezer container; place container upside down in 2-quart microwavable casserole. Microwave on High 5 minutes; remove container. Cover and microwave on Medium (50%) 15 to 20 minutes, breaking up and stirring every 5 minutes, until hot.

Creamy Potato Salad

Look for Dijon mustard–mayonnaise blends in the condiment section of your supermarket.

> *1 pound small new potatoes (about 12), cut in half*
> *1 package (10 ounces) frozen cut green beans*
> *¼ cup sliced green onions (2 to 3 medium)*
> *⅓ cup sour cream*
> *¼ cup Dijon mustard–mayonnaise blend*
> *1 tablespoon milk*
> *⅛ teaspoon lemon pepper*
> *2 hard-cooked eggs, peeled and cut into wedges*

Heat 1 inch water (salted if desired) to boiling in 2-quart saucepan. Add potatoes. Cover and heat to boiling; reduce heat. Simmer 10 minutes. Stir in frozen beans. Cover and heat to boiling; reduce heat. Simmer 8 to 9 minutes longer or until vegetables are tender; drain.

Place vegetables in medium glass bowl. Stir in onions. Mix remaining ingredients except eggs; fold into potato mixture. Carefully stir in egg wedges. See **TO STORE** and **TO SERVE**. *6 servings, about ¾ cup each.*

Per Serving: Calories 155; Protein 5 g; Carbohydrate 19 g (Dietary Fiber 3 g); Fat 8 g (Unsaturated 5 g, Saturated 3 g); Cholesterol 80 mg; Sodium 130 mg. Percent of U.S. RDA: Vitamin A 6%; Vitamin C 4%; Calcium 6%; Iron 8%.

TO STORE

Refrigerator: Cover and refrigerate at least 4 hours but no longer than 48 hours.

TO SERVE FROM REFRIGERATOR

Stir before serving (stir in small amount of additional milk, if necessary, to make dressing creamy).

Twice-baked Potatoes

4 large baking potatoes
¼ to ½ cup milk
¼ cup (½ stick) margarine or butter,
*   softened*
¼ teaspoon salt
Dash of pepper
1 cup shredded Cheddar cheese
*   (4 ounces)*
1 tablespoon chopped fresh chives

Heat oven to 350°. Prick potatoes several times with fork to allow steam to escape. Bake 1¼ to 1½ hours or until soft. (Or follow directions for microwaving potatoes, below.)

Cut thin slice from top of each potato; scoop out inside, leaving a thin shell. Mash potato in medium bowl until no lumps remain. Add small amounts of milk, beating after each addition. (Amount of milk needed to make potato smooth and fluffy depends on kind of potatoes.) Add margarine, salt and pepper; beat vigorously until potato is light and fluffy. Stir in cheese and chives. Fill potato shells with mashed potato. STOP HERE—see **To Store** and **To Reheat.**

To serve now, increase oven temperature to 400°. Bake on ungreased cookie sheet about 20 minutes or until hot. *4 servings.*

Microwave: Prick potatoes several times with fork to allow steam to escape. Arrange potatoes about 1 inch apart in circle on microwavable paper towel in microwave oven. Microwave uncovered on High 12 to 14 minutes, turning potatoes over after 6 minutes, until tender. Let stand 5 minutes. Prepare potatoes as directed above. Arrange filled potatoes in circle on 10-inch microwavable plate. Cover loosely and microwave on High 8 to 10 minutes, rotating plate ½ turn after 5 minutes, until hot.

> **Per Serving:** Calories 345; Protein 10 g; Carbohydrate 31 g (Dietary Fiber 2 g); Fat 21 g (Unsaturated 8 g, Saturated 13 g); Cholesterol 60 mg; Sodium 400 mg. Percent of U.S. RDA: Vitamin A 16%; Vitamin C 10%; Calcium 18%; Iron 4%.

TO STORE

Refrigerator: Refrigerate filled potatoes tightly covered no longer than 48 hours.

Freezer: Place filled potatoes in labeled airtight freezer container. Freeze no longer than 2 months.

TO REHEAT FROM REFRIGERATOR

Oven: About 40 minutes before serving, heat oven to 400°. Uncover and bake on ungreased cookie sheet about 30 minutes or until hot.

Microwave: About 15 minutes before serving, arrange refrigerated potatoes in circle on 10-inch microwavable plate. Cover loosely and microwave on High 12 to 15 minutes, rotating plate ½ turn after 5 minutes, until hot.

TO REHEAT FROM FREEZER

Oven: About 50 minutes before serving, heat oven to 400°. Bake uncovered on ungreased cookie sheet about 40 minutes or until hot.

Microwave: About 25 minutes before serving, arrange frozen potatoes in circle on 10-inch microwavable plate. Cover with plastic wrap, folding back 2-inch edge to vent. Microwave on High 10 minutes, rotating plate ½ turn after 5 minutes. Remove wrap and microwave 5 to 10 minutes longer, rotating plate ½ turn after 5 minutes, until hot.

Twice-baked Potatoes

Sweet Potato Clouds

These no-fuss potatoes are perfect for holiday meals when you have lots of other last-minute preparation.

> *3 large sweet potatoes (about 2 pounds),*
> *peeled and cut into 1-inch pieces*
> *¼ cup (½ stick) margarine or butter,*
> *softened*
> *2 tablespoons packed brown sugar*
> *½ teaspoon grated orange peel*
> *¼ teaspoon ground cardamom*
> *2 eggs, beaten*

To Complete Recipe:
> *1 tablespoon margarine or butter, melted*

Heat enough water to cover sweet potatoes (salted if desired) to boiling. Add potatoes. Cover and heat to boiling; reduce heat. Simmer about 20 minutes or until tender; drain. Shake potatoes in saucepan over low heat to dry. Mash potatoes until no lumps remain. Add remaining ingredients except 1 tablespoon margarine. Beat vigorously until potatoes are fluffy.

Drop potatoes by ½ cupfuls onto ungreased cookie sheet, forming 8 mounds. Or spoon potatoes into decorating bag and form 8 rosettes on ungreased cookie sheet. (If planning to freeze, cover cookie sheet with waxed paper.) STOP HERE—see **To Store** and **To Cook.**

To complete recipe and serve now, heat oven to 425°. Brush potatoes with 1 tablespoon margarine. Bake about 15 minutes or until hot. *8 servings.*

Per Serving: Calories 175; Protein 3 g; Carbohydrate 25 g (Dietary Fiber 2 g); Fat 8 g (Unsaturated 6 g, Saturated 2 g); Cholesterol 55 mg; Sodium 110 mg. Percent of U.S. RDA: Vitamin A 100%; Vitamin C 20%; Calcium 4%; Iron 4%.

To Store

Refrigerator: Cover tightly and refrigerate no longer than 24 hours.

Freezer: Freeze uncovered about 45 minutes or until firm. Place in labeled airtight freezer container. Freeze no longer than 2 months.

To Cook from Refrigerator

Oven: About 25 minutes before serving, heat oven to 425°. Brush potatoes with 1 tablespoon margarine. Bake about 12 minutes or until hot.

To Cook from Freezer

Oven: About 40 minutes before serving, heat oven to 375°. Grease cookie sheet. Place potato mounds on cookie sheet. Brush potatoes with 1 tablespoon margarine. Bake 25 to 30 minutes or until hot.

Crunchy Coleslaw

3 tablespoons sugar
2 tablespoons all-purpose flour
1 teaspoon ground mustard
½ teaspoon salt
⅛ teaspoon ground red pepper (cayenne)
1 egg
¾ cup water
¼ cup lemon juice
1 tablespoon margarine or butter
¼ to ½ cup sour cream
1 pound green cabbage, shredded or
  finely chopped (about 6 cups)
1 medium carrot, shredded (about ⅔ cup)
1 small green bell pepper, finely chopped
  (about ½ cup)

Mix sugar, flour, mustard, salt and red pepper in heavy 1-quart saucepan; beat in egg. Gradually stir in water and lemon juice until well blended. Cook over low heat 13 to 15 minutes, stirring constantly, until thickened and smooth; remove from heat. Stir in margarine until melted.

Place plastic wrap directly on surface of dressing; refrigerate about 2 hours or until cool. Stir in sour cream. Mix dressing and remaining ingredients. See **To Store** and **To Serve.** *8 servings, about ¾ cup each.*

Microwave: Mix sugar, flour, mustard, salt and red pepper in 1-quart microwavable casserole (do not beat in egg). Decrease water to ⅔ cup. Gradually stir in water and lemon juice until well blended. Microwave uncovered on High 2 to 3 minutes, stirring every minute, until thickened. Beat egg with hand beater until well blended. Stir about half of the hot mixture vigorously into beaten egg; pour mixture back into casserole, stirring until well blended. Microwave uncovered on Medium-high (70%) 1½ to 2 minutes, stirring after 1 minute, until thickened and smooth. Stir in margarine until melted. Continue as directed above.

Per Serving: Calories 85; Protein 2 g; Carbohydrate 11 g (Dietary Fiber 1 g); Fat 4 g (Unsaturated 2 g, Saturated 2 g); Cholesterol 35 mg; Sodium 170 mg. Percent of U.S. RDA: Vitamin A 18%; Vitamin C 40%; Calcium 4%; Iron 2%.

To Store

Refrigerator: Refrigerate tightly covered at least 1 hour but no longer than 24 hours.

To Serve from Refrigerator

Serve on salad greens if desired.

Marinated Corn and Peas

You can substitute a package of frozen cut asparagus or cut green beans for the peas. And for a new twist, substitute 1 can kidney beans (about 16 ounces), rinsed and drained, for the peas.

> *⅓ cup white wine vinegar*
> *1 tablespoon chopped fresh or 1 teaspoon dried thyme leaves*
> *1 tablespoon chopped fresh or 1 teaspoon dried basil leaves*
> *2 tablespoons vegetable oil*
> *¼ teaspoon salt*
> *⅛ teaspoon pepper*
> *1 package (10 ounces) frozen whole kernel corn, thawed and drained*
> *1 package (10 ounces) frozen green peas, thawed and drained*
> *1 cup cubed mozzarella cheese (4 ounces)*

To Complete Recipe:
> *Lettuce leaves*

Mix vinegar, thyme, basil, oil, salt and pepper in medium bowl. Stir in corn, peas and cheese. See **TO STORE** and **TO SERVE**. *6 servings, about ⅔ cup each.*

Per Serving: Calories 175; Protein 10 g; Carbohydrate 17 g (Dietary Fiber 4 g); Fat 9 g (Unsaturated 6 g, Saturated 3 g); Cholesterol 15 mg; Sodium 250 mg. Percent of U.S. RDA: Vitamin A 10%; Vitamin C 4%; Calcium 20%; Iron 8%.

TO STORE

Refrigerator: Cover tightly and refrigerate at least 2 hours but no longer than 48 hours.

TO SERVE FROM REFRIGERATOR

Spoon onto lettuce leaves, using slotted spoon.

Pasta-Bean Salad

> *1 cup uncooked medium shell macaroni*
> *2 medium stalks celery, sliced (about 1 cup)*
> *1 can (15 to 16 ounces) kidney beans, rinsed and drained*
> *1 cup cubed Cheddar cheese (4 ounces)*
> *¾ cup red wine vinegar*
> *1½ tablespoons chopped fresh or 1½ teaspoons dried tarragon leaves*
> *1 tablespoon sugar*
> *2 tablespoons olive or vegetable oil*
> *⅛ teaspoon red pepper sauce*

Cook macaroni as directed on package; drain. Rinse in cold water; drain. Mix macaroni and remaining ingredients in large glass bowl. See **TO STORE** and **TO SERVE**. *6 servings, about ¾ cup each.*

Per Serving: Calories 280; Protein 13 g; Carbohydrate 33 g (Dietary Fiber 5 g); Fat 13 g (Unsaturated 8 g, Saturated 5 g); Cholesterol 25 mg; Sodium 370 mg. Percent of U.S. RDA: Vitamin A 4%; Vitamin C *; Calcium 14%; Iron 16%.

TO STORE

Refrigerator: Cover and refrigerate at least 2 hours but no longer than 48 hours. Stir before serving.

TO SERVE FROM REFRIGERATOR

Stir before serving.

Confetti Pasta Salad

A little shredded Cheddar or Swiss cheese adds a flavorful touch to this colorful salad.

> *4 ounces rotini macaroni, cooked and chilled (about 2½ cups)*
> *1 medium carrot, thinly sliced (about ½ cup)*
> *½ cup shredded zucchini*
> *¼ cup sliced ripe olives*
> *¼ cup sliced green onions (2 to 3 medium)*
> *2 tablespoons chopped pimientos*
> *⅓ cup cider vinegar*
> *2 tablespoons packed brown sugar*
> *2 tablespoons water*
> *½ teaspoon celery seed*
> *½ teaspoon salt*
> *¼ teaspoon pepper*

Mix macaroni, carrot, zucchini, olives, onions and pimientos in large glass bowl. Shake remaining ingredients in tightly covered container. Pour over macaroni mixture; toss. See **TO STORE** and **TO SERVE**. *4 servings, about 1 cup each.*

Per Serving: Calories 160; Protein 4 g; Carbohydrate 33 g (Dietary Fiber 2 g); Fat 2 g (Unsaturated 2 g, Saturated 0 g); Cholesterol 0 mg; Sodium 590 mg. Percent of U.S. RDA: Vitamin A 30%; Vitamin C 6%; Calcium 4%; Iron 10%.

TO STORE

Refrigerator: Cover and refrigerate at least 1 hour but no longer than 48 hours.

TO SERVE FROM REFRIGERATOR

Stir before serving.

◫◫◫◫◫◫◫◫◫◫◫◫◫◫◫◫◫◫◫◫◫◫◫◫◫◫

3
Make-Ahead Menus for Friends

Feast for 4 (page 101)

Caesar Salad

Caesar Dressing (right)
1 large or 2 small bunches romaine, torn
into bite-size pieces (about 10 cups)

To Complete Recipe:
1 clove garlic, cut in half
1 cup garlic-flavored croutons
⅓ cup grated Parmesan cheese

Prepare Caesar Dressing. STOP HERE—see **To Store** and **To Serve.**

To complete recipe and serve now, rub large wooden salad bowl with cut clove of garlic. Allow a few small pieces of garlic to remain in bowl if desired. Add romaine and dressing; toss until leaves are coated. Sprinkle with croutons and cheese; toss. *8 servings, about 1⅓ cups each.*

CAESAR DRESSING

8 anchovy fillets, cut up
⅓ cup olive or vegetable oil
3 tablespoons lemon juice
1 teaspoon Worcestershire sauce
¼ teaspoon salt
¼ teaspoon ground mustard
Freshly ground pepper

Shake all ingredients in tightly covered container.

Per Serving: Calories 135; Protein 4g; Carbohydrate 6g (Dietary Fiber 1g); Fat 11g (Unsaturated 9g, Saturated 2g); Cholesterol 10mg; Sodium 320mg. Percent of U.S. RDA: Vitamin A 16%; Vitamin C 12%; Calcium 8%; Iron 6%.

TO STORE

Refrigerator: Place romaine in plastic bag; seal bag and refrigerate no longer than 24 hours. Refrigerate Caesar Dressing tightly covered no longer than 1 week.

TO SERVE FROM REFRIGERATOR

About 10 minutes before serving, rub large wooden salad bowl with cut clove of garlic. Allow a few small pieces of garlic to remain in bowl if desired. Add romaine and dressing; toss until leaves are coated. Sprinkle with croutons and cheese; toss.

Beef Burgundy

Serve plenty of bread to soak up the sauce.

2 tablespoons margarine or butter
5 medium onions, sliced
6 cups sliced mushrooms (about
*   1 pound)*
3 pounds beef stew meat, cut into 1-inch
*   cubes*
2 cloves garlic, minced
2 teaspoons salt
1 teaspoon chopped fresh or ¹/₂ teaspoon
*   dried marjoram leaves*
1 teaspoon chopped fresh or ¹/₂ teaspoon
*   dried thyme leaves*
¹/₄ teaspoon pepper
3 cups beef broth
3 tablespoons all-purpose flour
3¹/₂ cups red Burgundy

To Complete Recipe:
   Crusty French bread, if desired

Heat margarine in Dutch oven or 3-quart saucepan over medium heat until melted. Cook onions and mushrooms in margarine about 10 minutes, stirring occasionally, until onions are tender. Remove vegetables from Dutch oven; drain and reserve.

Cook beef and garlic in Dutch oven over medium heat, stirring occasionally, until beef is brown; drain. Sprinkle with salt, marjoram, thyme and pepper. Mix broth and flour; pour over beef. Heat to boiling, stirring constantly. Boil and stir 1 minute. Stir in Burgundy. Cover and simmer 1¹/₂ to 2 hours, stirring in onions and mushrooms 5 minutes before end of simmer time. STOP HERE—see **To Store** and **To Reheat**.

To complete recipe and serve now, spoon into bowls. Dip bread into sauce. *Enough for 2 meals of 4 (1-cup) servings each.*

> **Per Serving:** Calories 465; Protein 31 g; Carbohydrate 13 g (Dietary Fiber 2 g); Fat 33 g (Unsaturated 20 g, Saturated 13 g); Cholesterol 100 mg; Sodium 890 mg. Percent of U.S. RDA: Vitamin A 4%; Vitamin C *; Calcium 4%; Iron 24%.

To Store

Refrigerator: Cover tightly and refrigerate no longer than 4 days.

Freezer: Cool quickly (see page 7). Divide beef mixture between 2 labeled airtight 2-quart freezer containers. Freeze no longer than 2 months.

To Reheat from Refrigerator:

Stovetop: About 15 minutes before serving, heat 6 cups of the beef mixture uncovered in 2-quart saucepan over medium heat 8 to 10 minutes, stirring occasionally, until hot.

Microwave: About 15 minutes before serving, place 6 cups of the refrigerated beef mixture in 2-quart microwavable casserole. Cover tightly and microwave on High 8 to 10 minutes, stirring after 3 minutes, until hot.

To Reheat from Freezer

Stovetop: About 35 minutes before serving, dip 1 container into hot water to loosen; remove container. Heat ¹/₂ cup water and the beef mixture uncovered in 3-quart saucepan over medium heat 25 to 30 minutes, turning and stirring occasionally, until hot.

Microwave: About 25 minutes before serving, remove lid from 1 freezer container; place container upside down in 2-quart microwavable casserole. Microwave on High 5 minutes; remove container. Cover and microwave 15 to 20 minutes longer, breaking up and stirring every 5 minutes, until hot.

Pork-Onion Stroganoff

1½ pounds pork boneless loin
1 tablespoon margarine or butter
8 ounces mushrooms, sliced (about 3
    cups)
3 medium onions, sliced
1 clove garlic, finely chopped
1 tablespoon margarine or butter
1 cup beef broth
1½ tablespoons chopped fresh or 1½
    teaspoons dried basil leaves
1 tablespoon Worcestershire sauce
⅛ teaspoon pepper

To Complete Recipe:
    1 cup sour cream
    3 tablespoons all-purpose flour
    2 medium tomatoes, peeled, seeded and
        chopped (about 1½ cups)
    6 cups hot cooked noodles

Cut pork across grain into thin slices; cut slices into strips, each about 2½ × ½ inch. (For ease in cutting, partially freeze pork about 2 hours.) Heat 1 tablespoon margarine in 10-inch skillet over medium heat until bubbly. Cook mushrooms, onions and garlic in margarine, stirring frequently, until mushrooms and onions are tender. Remove mushroom mixture from skillet.

Heat 1 tablespoon margarine in skillet over medium-high heat until melted. Cook pork in margarine, stirring frequently, until brown. Stir in broth, basil, Worcestershire sauce and pepper. Heat to boiling; reduce heat. Cover and simmer about 10 minutes, stirring occasionally, until pork is tender. Stir in mushroom mixture. STOP HERE—see **To Store** and **To Reheat.**

To complete recipe and serve now, mix sour cream and flour; stir into pork mixture. Heat to boiling, stirring constantly. Boil and stir 1 minute. Stir in tomatoes; heat through. Serve over noodles. *6 servings, about 1⅔ cups each.*

Per Serving: Calories 650; Protein 36 g; Carbohydrate 37 g (Dietary Fiber 5 g); Fat 42 g (Unsaturated 26 g, Saturated 16 g); Cholesterol 145 mg; Sodium 380 mg. Percent of U.S. RDA: Vitamin A 14%; Vitamin C 10%; Calcium 8%; Iron 24%.

TO STORE

Refrigerator: Refrigerate pork mixture tightly covered no longer than 48 hours.

Freezer: Cool pork mixture 30 minutes. Place in labeled airtight 2-quart freezer container. Freeze no longer than 2 months.

TO REHEAT FROM REFRIGERATOR

Stovetop: About 25 minutes before serving, cover and heat pork mixture to boiling in 3-quart saucepan over medium heat, stirring frequently. Mix sour cream and flour; stir into pork mixture. Heat to boiling, stirring constantly. Boil and stir 1 minute. Stir in tomatoes; heat through. Serve over noodles.

Microwave: About 25 minutes before serving, place refrigerated pork mixture in 2-quart microwavable casserole. Cover and microwave on Medium (50%) 12 to 15 minutes, stirring every 4 minutes, until hot. Mix sour cream and flour; stir into pork mixture. Cover and microwave on Medium (50%) about 10 minutes, stirring every 4 minutes, until thickened. Stir in tomatoes. Microwave on Medium (50%) 3 to 5 minutes until tomatoes are hot. Serve over noodles.

TO REHEAT FROM FREEZER

Stovetop: About 30 minutes before serving, dip container into hot water to loosen; remove container. Cover and heat to boiling in 3-quart saucepan over medium heat, turning and stirring frequently. Mix sour cream and flour; stir into pork mixture. Heat to boiling, stirring constantly. Boil and stir 1 minute. Stir in tomatoes; heat through. Serve over noodles.

Microwave: About 40 minutes before serving, remove lid from freezer container; place container upside down in 2-quart microwavable casserole. Microwave on High 5 minutes; remove container. Cover and microwave on Medium (50%) 15 minutes; break up and stir. Cover and microwave on Medium (50%) 10 to 15 minutes longer, stirring every 5 minutes, until hot. Mix sour cream and flour; stir into pork mixture. Cover and microwave on Medium (50%) about 10 minutes, stirring 2 or 3 times, until thickened. Stir in tomatoes. Microwave on Medium (50%) 3 to 5 minutes until tomatoes are hot. Serve over noodles.

Mandarin Salad

You can make the salad dressing and candied almonds up to a week ahead of time—just be sure no one helps him- or herself to the almonds! To make extra candied almonds, cook 1 cup sliced almonds and ¼ cup sugar in a 10-inch skillet.

¼ cup sliced almonds
1 tablespoon plus 1 teaspoon sugar
Sweet-Sour Dressing (right)
¼ head lettuce, torn into bite-size pieces
¼ bunch romaine, torn into bite-size pieces
2 medium stalks celery, chopped (about 1 cup)
2 green onions, thinly sliced
1 can (11 ounces) mandarin orange segments, drained

Cook almonds and sugar over low heat in 1-quart saucepan, stirring constantly, until sugar is melted and almonds are coated; cool and break apart. Prepare Sweet-Sour Dressing. STOP HERE—see **To Store** and **To Serve.**

To serve now, place lettuce, romaine, celery, onions, orange segments and candied almonds in salad bowl. Pour Sweet-Sour Dressing over top; toss. *6 servings, about 1⅓ cups each.*

Sweet-Sour Dressing

¼ cup vegetable oil
2 tablespoons sugar
2 tablespoons white vinegar
1 tablespoon chopped fresh parsley
½ teaspoon salt
Dash of pepper
Dash of red pepper sauce

Shake all ingredients in tightly covered container.

Per Serving: Calories 175; Protein 2 g; Carbohydrate 16 g (Dietary Fiber 1 g); Fat 12 g (Unsaturated 10 g, Saturated 2 g); Cholesterol 0 mg; Sodium 200 mg. Percent of U.S. RDA: Vitamin A 4%; Vitamin C 26%; Calcium 4%; Iron 4%.

To Store

Refrigerator: Place lettuce, romaine, celery and onions in plastic bag; seal bag and refrigerate no longer than 24 hours. Refrigerate Sweet-Sour Dressing tightly covered no longer than 1 week. Store candied almonds covered at room temperature no longer than 1 week.

To Serve from Refrigerator

About 10 minutes before serving, pour dressing into bag of lettuce mixture; add orange segments. Close bag tightly and shake until salad greens and orange segments are well coated. Add almonds; close bag tightly and shake.

Birthday Bash for 6 (page 86)

Cherry-Lemon Cake Dessert

3 eggs
1 cup granulated sugar
¼ cup water
2 tablespoons lemon juice
¾ cup all-purpose flour
1 teaspoon baking powder
½ teaspoon grated lemon peel
½ cup cherry or strawberry preserves
½ cup granulated sugar
1½ teaspoons unflavored gelatin
2 egg yolks
½ cup water
⅓ cup lemon juice
¾ teaspoon grated lemon peel
2 cups whipping (heavy) cream
2 tablespoons powdered sugar
1 teaspoon vanilla

To Complete Recipe:
2 tablespoons sliced almonds, toasted

Heat oven to 375°. Line jelly roll pan, 15½ × 10½ × 1 inch, with cooking parchment paper, aluminum foil or waxed paper; grease aluminum foil or waxed paper generously. Beat eggs in small bowl on high speed about 5 minutes or until very thick and lemon colored. Pour eggs into medium bowl. Gradually beat in 1 cup granulated sugar on medium speed. Beat in ¼ cup water and 2 tablespoons lemon juice on low speed. Gradually add flour, baking powder and ½ teaspoon lemon peel, beating just until batter is smooth. Pour into pan, spreading to corners.

Bake 12 to 15 minutes or until toothpick inserted in center comes out clean. Immediately loosen cake from edges of pan and invert onto wire rack. Carefully remove paper. Cool cake completely. Cut cake crosswise into two 10½ × 7¾-inch rectangles. Spread preserves over 1 cake half. Stack second cake half on top. Cut cake stack into 1¼-inch squares.

Mix ⅓ cup granulated sugar and the gelatin in 1-quart saucepan. Stir in egg yolks, ½ cup water and ⅓ cup lemon juice. Cook over medium heat, stirring constantly, just until mixture boils. Stir in ¾ teaspoon lemon peel. Place saucepan in bowl of ice and water or refrigerate, stirring occasionally, until mixture mounds slightly when dropped from a spoon. Beat 1 cup of the whipping cream in chilled medium bowl until stiff. Fold whipped cream into lemon mixture.

Place half of the cake squares in large glass bowl. Spoon half of the whipped cream mixture over cake squares. Repeat with remaining cake squares and whipped cream mixture. Beat remaining 1 cup whipping cream, the powdered sugar and vanilla in chilled medium bowl until stiff. Spread over dessert. See **To Store** and **To Serve**. *10 servings.*

Per Serving: Calories 400; Protein 5 g; Carbohydrate 48 g (Dietary Fiber 0 g); Fat 21 g (Unsaturated 9 g, Saturated 12 g); Cholesterol 170 mg; Sodium 85 mg. Percent of U.S. RDA: Vitamin A 18%; Vitamin C *; Calcium 8%; Iron 4%.

To Store

Refrigerator: Cover tightly and refrigerate at least 6 hours but no longer than 48 hours.

To Serve from Refrigerator

Sprinkle with almonds.

SPICY FRUIT PUNCH*

BARBECUED BEEF SANDWICHES*

POTATO CHIPS

VEGETABLE RELISHES WITH DIP

CHOCOLATE CHIP–PEANUT FROZEN YOGURT
(SEE PAGE 160)

*Recipe follows

Spicy Fruit Punch

This chilled punch can be served with or without ice cubes. If you'd like to use ice cubes, make them out of apple cider or white grape juice so the punch isn't diluted. For an alcoholic punch, add ½ to 1 cup rum, brandy or vodka before serving.

> *3 cups apple cider*
> *2 teaspoons whole cloves*
> *3 three-inch sticks cinnamon*
> *2½ cups orange juice*
> *2½ cups dry white wine or white grape juice*

To Complete Recipe:
> *1½ cups frozen unsweetened raspberries*

Heat apple cider, cloves and cinnamon to boiling in 2-quart saucepan; reduce heat. Cover and simmer 15 minutes. Remove from heat; cool 15 minutes. Pour cider mixture into 2½-quart glass pitcher. Stir in orange juice and grape juice. See **TO STORE** and **TO SERVE**. *8 servings, about 1 cup each.*

Per Serving: Calories 145; Protein 1 g; Carbohydrate 35 g (Dietary Fiber 2 g); Fat 1 g (Unsaturated 1 g, Saturated 0 g); Cholesterol 0 mg; Sodium 5 mg. Percent of U.S. RDA: Vitamin A *; Vitamin C 50%; Calcium 2%; Iron 4%.

TO STORE

Refrigerator: Cover tightly and refrigerate at least 4 hours but no longer than 1 week.

TO SERVE FROM REFRIGERATOR

About 10 minutes before serving, strain punch to remove cloves and cinnamon. Stir in raspberries.

Barbecued Beef Sandwiches

Like your barbecue "hot"? Add a few dashes of red pepper sauce for extra kick.

*2½- to 3-pound beef boneless chuck pot
   roast*
1½ cups spicy eight-vegetable juice
1 medium onion, sliced
2 bay leaves
½ cup ketchup
2 tablespoons honey
1 tablespoon prepared mustard
½ cup beer or beef broth
2 tablespoons cornstarch

To Complete Recipe:
   8 frankfurter buns

Place beef roast in Dutch oven. Add vegetable juice, onion and bay leaves. Heat to boiling; reduce heat. Cover and simmer about 2 hours or until beef is tender.

Remove bay leaves. Drain beef, reserving 2 cups drippings. (Add additional vegetable juice to drippings if necessary to measure 2 cups.) Cut beef into thin slices. Mix 2 cups drippings, the ketchup, honey and mustard in Dutch oven. Heat to boiling.

Mix beer and cornstarch; stir into ketchup mixture. Heat to boiling. Boil and stir 1 minute or until mixture thickens. Stir in beef slices; heat through. STOP HERE—see **TO STORE** and **TO REHEAT.**

To complete recipe and serve now, spoon onto buns. *8 servings.*

After-the-Game Get-together for 8 (page 91)

Per Serving: Calories 640; Protein 37 g; Carbohydrate 37 g (Dietary Fiber 2 g); Fat 39 g (Unsaturated 24 g, Saturated 15 g); Cholesterol 120 mg; Sodium 670 mg. Percent of U.S. RDA: Vitamin A 6%; Vitamin C 10%; Calcium 8%; Iron 24%.

TO STORE

Refrigerator: Refrigerate tightly covered no longer than 48 hours.

Freezer: Cool beef mixture 30 minutes. Place in labeled airtight 2-quart freezer container. Freeze no longer than 2 months.

TO REHEAT FROM REFRIGERATOR

Stovetop: About 15 minutes before serving, cover and heat in 3-quart saucepan over medium heat about 15 minutes, stirring frequently, until hot. Spoon onto buns.

Microwave: About 15 minutes before serving, place refrigerated beef mixture in 2-quart microwavable casserole. Cover and microwave on Medium (50%) 13 to 15 minutes, stirring frequently, until hot. Spoon onto buns.

TO REHEAT FROM FREEZER

Stovetop: About 1 hour before serving, dip container into hot water to loosen; remove container. Cover and heat in 3-quart saucepan over medium-low heat about 55 minutes, turning and stirring frequently, until hot. Spoon onto buns.

Microwave: About 40 minutes before serving, remove lid from freezer container; place container upside down in 2-quart microwavable casserole. Microwave on High 5 minutes; remove container. Cover and microwave on Medium (50%) 20 minutes; break up and stir. Cover and microwave on Medium (50%) about 10 minutes longer, stirring after 5 minutes, until hot. Spoon onto buns.

WINTER SOUP SUPPER FOR 4

MEATBALL-VEGETABLE SOUP* OR
TOMATO-BEAN SOUP*

CARROT AND CELERY STICKS

HARD ROLLS

APPLE PIE (SEE PAGE 145) WITH
CHEDDAR CHEESE

Recipe follows

Meatball-Vegetable Soup

1 pound ground beef
1 cup soft whole wheat bread crumbs
(about 1½ slices bread)
½ teaspoon onion powder
½ teaspoon chili powder
1 egg
4 cups beef broth
1 tablespoon chopped fresh or 1 teaspoon
dried cilantro leaves
¼ teaspoon pepper
2 medium carrots, sliced (about 1 cup)
1 medium onion, chopped (about ½ cup)
1 package (10 ounces) frozen mixed
vegetables

Heat oven to 400°. Mix ground beef, bread crumbs, onion powder, chili powder and egg. Shape mixture into 24 meatballs. Place in ungreased rectangular pan, 13 × 9 × 2 inches. Bake uncovered 20 to 25 minutes or until no longer pink in center; drain well.

Meanwhile, mix remaining ingredients in 3-quart saucepan. Heat to boiling; reduce heat. Cover and simmer about 20 minutes, stirring occasionally, until hot. STOP HERE—see **TO STORE** and **TO REHEAT.**

To serve now, stir meatballs into broth mixture. Cover and simmer 20 minutes longer, stirring occasionally. *4 servings, about 1½ cups each.*

Per Serving: Calories 345; Protein 29 g; Carbohydrate 18 g; (Dietary Fiber 4 g); Fat 19 g (Unsaturated 12 g, Saturated 7 g); Cholesterol 125 mg; Sodium 830 mg. Percent of U.S. RDA: Vitamin A 100%; Vitamin C 20%; Calcium 8%; Iron 20%.

TO STORE

Refrigerator: Stir meatballs into broth mixture. Refrigerate tightly covered no longer than 48 hours.

Freezer: Cool broth mixture 30 minutes; stir in meatballs. Place soup in labeled airtight 2-quart freezer container. Freeze no longer than 2 months.

TO REHEAT FROM REFRIGERATOR

Stovetop: About 30 minutes before serving, cover and heat soup to boiling in 3-quart saucepan over medium heat, stirring occasionally. Boil 2 minutes.

Microwave: About 35 minutes before serving, place refrigerated soup in 2-quart microwavable casserole. Cover tightly and microwave on High 10 to 12 minutes, stirring after 5 minutes, until meatballs are hot.

TO REHEAT FROM FREEZER

Stovetop: About 1 hour before serving, dip freezer container into hot water to loosen; remove container. Cover and heat to boiling in 3-quart saucepan over medium heat, turning and stirring frequently. Boil 2 minutes.

Microwave: About 35 minutes before serving, remove lid from freezer container; place container upside down in 2-quart microwavable casserole. Cover and microwave on Medium (50%) 25 minutes; remove container. Break up and stir. Cover and microwave on Medium (50%) about 20 minutes longer, stirring 2 or 3 times, until hot.

Tomato-Bean Soup

1 cup cubed fully cooked smoked ham
3 cups beef broth
1½ tablespoons chopped fresh or 1½ tea-
*   spoons dried basil leaves*
1 tablespoon chopped fresh or 1 teaspoon
*   dried marjoram leaves*
¼ teaspoon pepper
2 medium stalks celery, chopped (about 1
*   cup)*
1 medium onion, chopped (about ½ cup)
1 bay leaf
1 can (16 ounces) stewed tomatoes,
*   undrained*
1 can (15 to 16 ounces) kidney beans,
*   drained*
1 can (15 to 16 ounces) navy beans,
*   drained*
1 can (15 to 16 ounces) garbanzo beans,
*   drained*
1 can (15 to 16 ounces) black-eyed peas,
*   drained*

To Complete Recipe:
Grated Parmesan cheese, if desired

Mix all ingredients except cheese in Dutch oven. Cover and heat to boiling; reduce heat. Simmer 30 minutes, stirring occasionally. Remove bay leaf. STOP HERE—see **To Store** and **To Reheat.**

To complete recipe and serve now, serve with cheese. *8 servings, about 1 cup each.*

Per Serving: Calories 270; Protein 20 g; Carbohydrate 47 g (Dietary Fiber 13 g); Fat 6 g (Unsaturated 4 g, Saturated 2 g); Cholesterol 10 mg; Sodium 940 mg. Percent of U.S. RDA: Vitamin A 6%; Vitamin C 10%; Calcium 10%; Iron 30%.

To Store

Refrigerator: Refrigerate tightly covered no longer than 48 hours.

Freezer: Cool soup 30 minutes. Place soup in labeled airtight 2-quart freezer container. Freeze no longer than 2 months.

To Reheat from Refrigerator

Stovetop: About 30 minutes before serving, cover and heat soup to boiling in 3-quart saucepan over medium heat, stirring occasionally. Serve with cheese.

Microwave: About 15 minutes before serving, place refrigerated soup in 2½-quart microwavable casserole. Cover and microwave on High 12 to 14 minutes, stirring every 4 minutes, until hot. Serve with cheese.

To Reheat from Freezer

Stovetop: About 1 hour before serving, dip container into hot water to loosen; remove container. Cover and heat to boiling in 3-quart saucepan over medium heat, turning and stirring frequently. Serve with cheese.

Microwave: About 35 minutes before serving, remove lid from freezer container; place container upside down in 2½-quart microwavable casserole. Microwave on High 5 minutes; remove container. Cover and microwave on Medium (50%) 15 minutes; break up and stir. Cover and microwave on Medium (50%) about 15 minutes longer, stirring every 5 minutes, until hot. Serve with cheese.

Potato-Carrot Mounds

*6 medium potatoes (about 2 pounds),
   peeled and cut into fourths*
⅓ to ½ cup milk
2 eggs, beaten
*¼ cup (½ stick) margarine or butter,
   softened*
¼ cup shredded carrot
¼ teaspoon pepper

To Complete Recipe:
2 tablespoons margarine or butter, melted

Heat 1 inch water (salted if desired) to boiling in 3-quart saucepan. Add potatoes. Cover and heat to boiling; reduce heat. Simmer 30 to 35 minutes or until tender; drain. Shake potatoes in saucepan over low heat to dry. Mash potatoes until no lumps remain. Add milk in small amounts, beating after each addition (amount of milk needed to make potatoes smooth and fluffy depends on kind of potatoes used). Add eggs, ¼ cup margarine, the carrot and pepper. Beat vigorously until potatoes are light and fluffy.

Drop potatoes by spoonfuls onto ungreased cookie sheet, forming 8 mounds. Or spoon potatoes into decorating bag and form 8 rosettes on ungreased cookie sheet. (If planning to freeze, cover cookie sheet with waxed paper.) STOP HERE—see **To Store** and **To Cook**.

To complete recipe and serve now, heat oven to 425°. Brush potatoes with 2 tablespoons margarine. Bake about 15 minutes or until light brown. *8 servings, about ½ cup each.*

Per Serving: Calories 190; Protein 4 g; Carbohydrate 23 g (Dietary Fiber 2 g); Fat 10 g (Unsaturated 8 g, Saturated 2 g); Cholesterol 55 mg; Sodium 130 mg. Percent of U.S. RDA: Vitamin A 24%; Vitamin C 6%; Calcium 2%; Iron 8%.

TO STORE

Refrigerator: Cover unbaked potato mounds tightly and refrigerate no longer than 24 hours.

Freezer: Freeze unbaked potato mounds uncovered about 45 minutes or until firm. Place potato mounds in labeled airtight freezer container. Freeze no longer than 2 months.

TO COOK FROM REFRIGERATOR

Oven: About 25 minutes before serving, heat oven to 425°. Brush potatoes with 2 tablespoons margarine. Bake about 15 minutes or until light brown.

TO COOK FROM FREEZER

Oven: About 30 minutes before serving, heat oven to 375°. Grease cookie sheet. Place potato mounds on cookie sheet. Brush with 2 tablespoons margarine. Bake 20 to 25 minutes or until hot.

Whole Wheat Brown-and-Serve Rolls

If you prefer plain white rolls, use all-purpose flour in place of the whole wheat flour.

2 cups stone-ground whole wheat flour
¼ cup sugar
1 teaspoon salt
1 package regular or quick-acting active dry yeast
¾ cup very warm water (120° to 130°)
¾ cup very warm milk (120° to 130°)
¼ cup shortening
2½ cups all-purpose flour
Margarine or butter, softened

Mix whole wheat flour, sugar, salt and yeast in large bowl. Add water, milk and shortening. Beat on low speed 1 minute, scraping bowl frequently. Beat on medium speed 1 minute, scraping bowl frequently. Stir in enough all-purpose flour, 1 cup at a time, to make dough easy to handle.

Turn dough onto lightly floured surface; gently roll in flour to coat. Knead about 5 minutes or until smooth and elastic. Place in greased bowl; turn greased side up. Cover and let rise in warm place about 1½ hours or until double. (Dough is ready if indentation remains when touched.)

Punch down dough; turn onto lightly floured surface. Shape into Dinner Rolls or Parker House Rolls as directed below. Brush with margarine. Cover and let rise in warm place 35 to 40 minutes or until double.

Heat oven to 275°. Bake 20 to 30 minutes or until dry and set but not brown. Remove from pans to wire racks; cool to room temperature. STOP HERE—see **To Store** and **To Reheat**.

Holiday Dinner for 8 (page 97)

To serve now, heat oven to 400°. Bake 15 to 20 minutes or until golden brown. *24 rolls.*

Per Roll: Calories 115; Protein 3 g; Carbohydrate 20 g (Dietary Fiber 1 g); Fat 3 g (Unsaturated 2 g, Saturated 1 g); Cholesterol 5 mg; Sodium 100 mg. Percent of U.S. RDA: Vitamin A *; Vitamin C *; Calcium 2%; Iron 6%.

Dinner Rolls: Grease 24 medium muffin cups, 2½ × 1¼ inches, or 2 cookie sheets. Divide dough into 24 equal pieces. Shape each piece into smooth ball. Place in muffin cups or about 3 inches apart on cookie sheets.

Parker House Rolls: Grease 2 square pans, 9 × 9 × 2 inches. Divide dough in half. Flatten each half with hands or rolling pin into rectangle, 12 × 9 inches. Cut with floured 3-inch round cutter. Brush each circle with margarine. Make crease across each circle; fold so top half slightly overlaps bottom half. Press edges together. Place close together in pans.

To Store

Refrigerator: Wrap tightly and refrigerate no longer than 8 days.

Freezer: Wrap tightly and label. Freeze no longer than 2 months.

To Reheat from Refrigerator

Oven: About 20 minutes before serving, heat oven to 400°. Heat on ungreased cookie sheet 7 to 10 minutes or until brown and hot.

To Reheat from Freezer

Oven: About 25 minutes before serving, heat oven to 400°. Heat on ungreased cookie sheet 7 to 10 minutes or until brown and hot.

Frozen Pumpkin Dessert

⅔ cup all-purpose flour
⅓ cup chopped walnuts
⅓ cup margarine or butter, melted
2 tablespoons packed brown sugar
½ cup granulated sugar
1 envelope unflavored gelatin
1½ cups apple juice
½ teaspoon ground cinnamon
¼ teaspoon ground ginger
Dash of ground cloves
1 can (16 ounces) pumpkin
½ cup whipping (heavy) cream
Whipped cream, if desired
Cranberry sauce, if desired

Heat oven to 350°. Mix flour, walnuts, margarine and brown sugar. Spread in ungreased rectangular pan, 13 × 9 × 2 inches. Bake 18 to 20 minutes, stirring occasionally to break into a crumbly mixture, until golden brown. Cool slightly. Sprinkle two-thirds of the walnut mixture in ungreased square baking pan, 8 × 8 × 2 inches.

Mix granulated sugar and gelatin in 2-quart saucepan. Stir in apple juice, cinnamon, ginger and cloves. Cook over medium heat, stirring constantly, until gelatin is completely dissolved. Place saucepan in bowl of ice and water or refrigerate 20 to 30 minutes, stirring occasionally, just until mixture mounds slightly when dropped from a spoon. Fold pumpkin into gelatin mixture.

Beat whipping cream in chilled small bowl until stiff. Fold whipped cream into pumpkin mixture. Spoon evenly over walnut mixture in pan. Sprinkle remaining walnut mixture over top. See **TO STORE** and **TO SERVE**. *8 servings.*

Per Serving: Calories 295; Protein 3 g; Carbohydrate 36 g (Dietary Fiber 1 g); Fat 16 g (Unsaturated 11 g, Saturated 5 g); Cholesterol 20 mg; Sodium 100 mg. Percent of U.S. RDA: Vitamin A 100%; Vitamin C *; Calcium 4%; Iron 10%.

TO STORE

Freezer: Wrap tightly and label. Freeze at least 6 hours but no longer than 1 month.

TO SERVE FROM FREEZER

About 1 hour before serving, let stand covered at room temperature to soften, or place in refrigerator at least 4 hours but no longer than 8 hours before serving. Serve with whipped cream and cranberry sauce.

FEAST FOR 4

GINGERED APRICOT CHICKEN BREASTS*

RICE-FRUIT MEDLEY*

BUTTERED BROCCOLI SPEARS

BROWNIES WITH ICE CREAM AND
CARAMEL SAUCE

*Recipe follows

Gingered Apricot Chicken Breasts

If you are keeping tabs on your sodium intake, try this recipe with reduced-sodium soy sauce.

> *1 can (5½ ounces) apricot nectar*
> *2 tablespoons dry white wine or apricot nectar*
> *2 tablespoons soy sauce*
> *1 tablespoon vegetable oil*
> *1 teaspoon grated gingerroot or ¼ teaspoon ground ginger*
> *4 skinless boneless chicken breast halves (about 1 pound)*

To Complete Recipe:
> *2 teaspoons cornstarch*

Mix all ingredients except chicken breast halves and cornstarch in heavy-duty plastic food-storage bag. Add chicken, turning to coat. Seal tightly. See **TO STORE** and **TO COOK**. *4 servings.*

Per Serving: Calories 195; Protein 25 g; Carbohydrate 8 g (Dietary Fiber 0 g); Fat 7 g (Unsaturated 5 g, Saturated 2 g); Cholesterol 60 mg; Sodium 570 mg. Percent of U.S. RDA: Vitamin A 4%; Vitamin C *; Calcium 2%; Iron 8%.

TO STORE

Refrigerator: Refrigerate at least 1 hour but no longer than 24 hours.

Freezer: Label bag of chicken mixture. Freeze no longer than 2 months.

TO COOK FROM REFRIGERATOR

Oven: Heat oven to 375°. Grease square pan, 8 × 8 × 2 inches. Remove chicken from marinade; reserve marinade. Place chicken in pan. Bake uncovered about 20 minutes or until juice is no longer pink when centers of thickest pieces are cut. Mix marinade and cornstarch in 1-quart saucepan. Heat to boiling. Boil and stir 1 minute. Serve over chicken.

TO COOK FROM FREEZER

At least 12 hours before serving or overnight, place frozen chicken in refrigerator to thaw. Follow **TO COOK FROM REFRIGERATOR** directions.

Rice-Fruit Medley

If you like pine nuts or sunflower seeds, try them in this recipe in place of the pecans.

> *¾ cup uncooked brown rice*
> *⅓ cup diced dried fruit and raisin mixture*
> *¼ cup sliced green onions (2 to 3 medium)*
> *2¼ cups chicken broth*

To Complete Recipe:
> *¼ cup chopped pecans, toasted*

Mix all ingredients except pecans in 1½-quart saucepan. Heat to boiling; reduce heat. Cover and simmer about 45 minutes, stirring occasionally, until rice is tender and broth is absorbed. STOP HERE—see **To Store** and **To Reheat.**

To complete recipe and serve now, stir in pecans. *4 servings, about ½ cup each.*

Per Serving: Calories 225; Protein 7 g; Carbohydrate 37 g (Dietary Fiber 4 g); Fat 7 g (Unsaturated 6 g, Saturated 1 g); Cholesterol 0 mg; Sodium 450 mg. Percent of U.S. RDA: Vitamin A 2%; Vitamin C *; Calcium 2%; Iron 8%.

To Store

Refrigerator: Place rice mixture in 1½-quart casserole. (If planning to microwave, use microwavable casserole.) Cover and refrigerate no longer than 48 hours.

To Reheat from Refrigerator

Oven: About 35 minutes before serving, heat oven to 375°. Bake in covered casserole 20 to 25 minutes or until hot.

Microwave: About 10 minutes before serving, microwave covered casserole on High 4 to 6 minutes, stirring after 3 minutes, until hot.

BUSY WEEKNIGHT DINNER FOR 6

TOMATO-HAM BALLS*

BUTTERED PEAS

LETTUCE WEDGES WITH RANCH DRESSING

GERMAN CHOCOLATE PARFAITS*

*Recipe follows

Tomato-Ham Balls

These ham balls also make a zesty meatball sandwich—just spoon into hoagie buns or heroes.

> *¾ pound ground beef*
> *½ pound ground fully cooked smoked ham*
> *½ cup unseasoned dry bread crumbs*
> *⅓ cup finely chopped onion*
> *¼ cup milk*
> *1 tablespoon chopped fresh or 1 teaspoon dried marjoram leaves*
> *¼ teaspoon pepper*
> *1 egg*
> *1 can (11 ounces) condensed tomato bisque soup*
> *¼ cup water*
> *1 tablespoon packed brown sugar*
> *2 tablespoons white vinegar*
> *1 tablespoon prepared mustard*

To Complete Recipe:
> *6 cups hot cooked rice or pasta*

Heat oven to 400°. Mix ground beef, ground ham, bread crumbs, onion, milk, marjoram, pepper and egg. Shape mixture into twenty-four

1¼-inch balls. Place in ungreased rectangular pan, 13 × 9 × 2 inches. Bake 25 minutes; drain well. Mix remaining ingredients except rice. STOP HERE—see **To Store** and **To Reheat.**

To complete recipe and serve now, mix soup mixture and ham balls in 2-quart saucepan. Heat to boiling; reduce heat. Cover and simmer 15 minutes, stirring frequently. Serve over rice. *6 servings.*

Per Serving: Calories 695; Protein 24 g; Carbohydrate 75 g (Dietary Fiber 2 g); Fat 34 g (Unsaturated 25 g, Saturated 9 g); Cholesterol 95 mg; Sodium 1650 mg. Percent of U.S. RDA: Vitamin A 4%; Vitamin C 30%; Calcium 6%; Iron 32%.

To Store

Refrigerator: Stir ham balls into unheated soup mixture. Cover tightly and refrigerate no longer than 4 days.

Freezer: Stir ham balls into unheated soup mixture. Place in labeled airtight 1½-quart freezer container. Freeze no longer than 2 months.

To Reheat from Refrigerator

Stovetop: About 45 minutes before serving, cover and heat to boiling in 3-quart saucepan over medium heat, stirring frequently. Serve over rice.

Microwave: About 20 minutes before serving, place refrigerated ham mixture in 1½-quart microwavable casserole. Cover and microwave on Medium (50%) 10 minutes; stir. Cover and microwave on Medium (50%) 7 to 10 minutes longer, stirring 2 or 3 times, until hot. Serve over rice.

To Reheat from Freezer

Stovetop: About 45 minutes before serving, dip container into hot water to loosen; remove container. Cover and heat to boiling in 3-quart saucepan over medium-low heat, turning and stirring occasionally, being careful not to break up ham balls. Serve over rice.

Microwave: About 45 minutes before serving, remove lid from freezer container; place container upside down in 2-quart microwavable casserole. Microwave on High 5 minutes; remove container. Cover and microwave on Medium (50%) 15 minutes; break up and stir. Cover and microwave on Medium (50%) 13 to 15 minutes longer, stirring every 5 minutes and being careful not to break up ham balls, until hot. Serve over rice.

German Chocolate Parfaits

If you don't have parfait glasses, wine or champagne glasses work well for this luscious dessert.

>*½ cup sugar*
>*⅓ cup cocoa*
>*2 tablespoons cornstarch*
>*2 cups milk*
>*2 egg yolks, slightly beaten*
>*2 tablespoons margarine or butter, softened*
>*2 teaspoons vanilla*
>*1 bar (4 ounces) sweet cooking chocolate, chopped*
>*1 tablespoon shortening*
>*¼ cup coconut, toasted*
>*¼ cup chopped peanuts*

To Complete Recipe:
>*Whipped cream, if desired*

Mix sugar, cocoa and cornstarch in 2-quart saucepan. Gradually stir in milk. Cook over medium heat, stirring constantly, until mixture thickens and boils. Boil and stir 1 minute. Gradually stir at least half of the hot mixture into egg yolks; stir back into hot mixture in saucepan. Boil and stir 1 minute; remove from heat. Stir in margarine and vanilla. Place plastic wrap directly on surface of pudding. Refrigerate about 1 hour or until slightly chilled.

Mix chocolate and shortening in 1-quart heavy saucepan. Cook over low heat, stirring constantly, until chocolate is melted. Cool slightly. Mix coconut and peanuts. Divide one-third of pudding, chocolate mixture and coconut mixture among 4 parfait glasses. Repeat twice. STOP HERE—see **To Store** and **To Serve**.

To complete recipe and serve now, top each with dollop of whipped cream. *4 servings.*

Per Serving: Calories 570; Protein 11 g; Carbohydrate 57 g (Dietary Fiber 6 g); Fat 36 g (Unsaturated 20 g, Saturated 16 g); Cholesterol 115 mg; Sodium 200 mg. Percent of U.S. RDA: Vitamin A 18%; Vitamin C *; Calcium 22%; Iron 14%.

To Store

Refrigerator: Cover and refrigerate at least 2 hours but no longer than 48 hours.

To Serve from Refrigerator

Top each with dollop of whipped crean.

Pasta Supper for 6 (page 106)

PASTA SUPPER FOR 6

TURKEY-PASTA PIE*

TOSSED SALAD WITH ITALIAN DRESSING

HERBED WHOLE WHEAT BREADSTICKS
(SEE PAGE 138) OR PURCHASED BREADSTICKS

CITRUS-CHAMPAGNE SHERBET*

*Recipe follows

Turkey-Pasta Pie

½ pound ground turkey
1 small onion, finely chopped (about ¼ cup)
1 can (8 ounces) stewed tomatoes, undrained
1 can (8 ounces) tomato sauce
½ teaspoon Italian seasoning
6 ounces uncooked fettuccine
1 egg
1 tablespoon margarine or butter, melted
1 cup shredded mozzarella cheese (4 ounces)
1 cup small curd creamed cottage cheese
1 egg
1 cup chopped fresh broccoli or frozen (thawed) chopped broccoli
¼ cup grated Parmesan cheese

Cook ground turkey and onion in 10-inch skillet over medium heat, stirring frequently, until no longer pink; drain. Stir in tomatoes, tomato sauce and Italian seasoning. Heat to boiling; reduce heat. Cover and simmer 10 minutes, stirring occasionally.

Meanwhile, cook fettuccine as directed on package; drain. Beat 1 egg and the margarine in medium bowl. Stir in fettuccine and mozzarella cheese. Spoon mixture into ungreased pie plate, 10 × 1½ inches; press evenly on bottom and up side. Mix cottage cheese and 1 egg; spread over fettuccine mixture on bottom of pie plate. Sprinkle with broccoli. Spoon turkey mixture evenly over top. Sprinkle with Parmesan cheese. STOP HERE—see **To Store** and **To Cook.**

To serve now, heat oven to 350°. Bake uncovered about 30 minutes or until hot in center. Let stand 10 minutes before cutting. *6 servings.*

> **Per Serving:** Calories 345; Protein 26 g; Carbohydrate 29 g (Dietary Fiber 3 g); Fat 15 g (Unsaturated 11 g, Saturated 6 g); Cholesterol 140 mg; Sodium 820 mg. Percent of U.S. RDA: Vitamin A 20%; Vitamin C 20%; Calcium 24%; Iron 16%.

TO STORE

Refrigerator: Cover unbaked pie with aluminum foil and refrigerate no longer than 24 hours.

Freezer: Wrap unbaked pie tightly and label. Freeze no longer than 1 month.

TO COOK FROM REFRIGERATOR

Oven: About 1¼ hours before serving, heat oven to 350°. Bake in covered pie plate about 1 hour or until hot in center. Let stand for 10 minutes before cutting.

TO COOK FROM FREEZER

Oven: About 2¼ hours before serving, heat oven to 400°. Unwrap and cover with aluminum foil. Bake about 2 hours or until hot in center. Let stand for 10 minutes before cutting.

Citrus-Champagne Sherbet

1½ cups sugar
1 tablespoon unflavored gelatin
1 cup orange juice
2 cups champagne or white grape juice,
  or 1 cup of each
1 cup half-and-half
½ cup lemon juice
1 teaspoon grated orange peel
1 teaspoon grated lemon peel
1 or 2 drops yellow food color, if desired

Mix sugar and gelatin in 2-quart saucepan. Stir in orange juice. Heat over medium heat, stirring constantly, until sugar and gelatin are dissolved; remove from heat. Stir in remaining ingredients. Pour into square pan, 8 × 8 × 2 inches.

Cover and freeze 2 to 3 hours or until firm. Break frozen mixture into chunks and place in chilled bowl. Beat on low speed until no chunks remain. Return mixture to pan. See **To Store** and **To Serve.** *8 servings, about ½ cup each.*

Per Serving: Calories 255; Protein 2 g; Carbohydrate 44 g (Dietary Fiber 0 g); Fat 4 g (Unsaturated 2 g, Saturated 2 g); Cholesterol 10 mg; Sodium 25 mg. Percent of U.S. RDA: Vitamin A 2%; Vitamin C 28%; Calcium 4%; Iron 2%.

To Store

Freezer: Wrap tightly and freeze at least 6 hours but no longer than 1 month.

To Serve from Freezer

Scoop or spoon into champagne or sherbet glasses.

Scrambled Egg Stacks

This elegant breakfast is especially good when made with whole wheat English muffins. Sizes of English muffins can vary, so you may need the larger pan size listed.

> *4 English muffins, split and toasted*
> *16 very thin slices fully cooked smoked*
>   *ham*
> *Cheese Sauce (right)*
> *8 eggs*
> *½ cup milk*
> *1 teaspoon ground mustard*
> *½ teaspoon salt*
> *¼ teaspoon pepper*
> *2 tablespoons margarine or butter*

Grease rectangular baking dish, 13 × 9 × 2 inches, or jelly roll pan, 15 × 10 × 1 inch. Arrange muffin halves in dish. Layer 2 slices ham on each muffin half. Prepare Cheese Sauce.

Stir eggs, milk, mustard, salt and pepper thoroughly with fork for uniform yellow color, or stir slightly for streaks of white and yellow. Heat 2 tablespoons margarine in 10-inch skillet over medium heat until melted and hot. Pour egg mixture into skillet. As mixture begins to set at bottom and side, gently lift cooked portions with spatula so that thin, uncooked portion can flow to bottom. Avoid constant stirring. Cook 7 to 8 minutes or until eggs are thickened and cooked throughout but still moist. Spoon eggs evenly over muffins. STOP HERE—see **TO STORE** and **TO COOK.**

To serve now, heat oven to 350°. Spoon Cheese Sauce over egg stacks. Bake uncovered 8 to 10 minutes until hot. *8 servings.*

CHEESE SAUCE

> *2 tablespoons margarine or butter*
> *⅓ cup sliced green onions (about 3*
>   *medium)*
> *2 tablespoons all-purpose flour*
> *1½ tablespoons chopped fresh or 1½*
>   *teaspoons dried thyme leaves*
> *⅛ teaspoon pepper*
> *1 cup milk*
> *½ cup shredded Cheddar cheese (2*
>   *ounces)*

Heat margarine in 1½-quart saucepan over medium heat until melted. Cook onions in margarine, stirring frequently, until tender. Gradually stir in flour, thyme and pepper. Cook over medium heat, stirring constantly, until mixture is bubbly and thickened; remove from heat.

Stir in milk. Heat to boiling, stirring constantly. Boil and stir 1 minute. Stir in cheese until melted; remove from heat.

> **Per Serving:** Calories 295; Protein 18 g; Carbohydrate 18 g (Dietary Fiber 1 g); Fat 17 g (Unsaturated 11 g, Saturated 6 g); Cholesterol 240 mg; Sodium 900 mg. Percent of U.S. RDA: Vitamin A 20%; Vitamin C 6%; Calcium 18%; Iron 12%.

TO STORE

Refrigerator: Cover egg stacks tightly, place plastic wrap directly on surface of Cheese Sauce and refrigerate no longer than 24 hours.

TO COOK FROM REFRIGERATOR

Oven: About 30 minutes before serving, heat oven to 350°. Spoon Cheese Sauce over egg stacks. Bake uncovered about 20 minutes or until hot.

Two-Berry Ice

This fresh sorbet goes very well with specialty cookies, such as coconut macaroons or meringue cookies.

> *2 cups strawberry halves*
> *1 cup blueberries*
> *1 cup apple juice*
> *½ cup sugar*

Place all ingredients in blender. Cover and blend until smooth. Press mixture through sieve. Pour into loaf pan, 8½ × 4½ × 2½ inches. Cover and freeze 4 to 6 hours or until firm. Break frozen mixture into chunks and place in chilled bowl. Beat on low speed until no large chunks remain. Return mixture to pan. STOP HERE—see **TO STORE** and **TO SERVE**. *8 servings, about ½ cup each.*

> **Per Serving:** Calories 80; Protein 0 g; Carbohydrate 21 g (Dietary Fiber 1 g); Fat 0 g (Unsaturated 0 g, Saturated 0 g); Cholesterol 0 mg; Sodium 5 mg. Percent of U.S. RDA: Vitamin A *; Vitamin C 20%; Calcium *; Iron 2%.

TO STORE

Freezer: Wrap tightly and freeze at least 6 hours but no longer than 1 month.

TO SERVE FROM FREEZER

Scoop, spoon or cut into squares.

SALAD SAMPLER LUNCHEON FOR 8

FRUITED TURKEY SALAD*

WHITE BEAN SALAD*

PIÑA COLADA MOLD (SEE PAGE 112)

SEVEN-LAYER CHEF'S SALAD (SEE PAGE 57)

ASSORTED MUFFINS

*Recipe follows

Fruited Turkey Salad

You'll also find this salad delicious made with smoked turkey.

1 container (6 ounces) lemon, peach or
orange yogurt (about ⅔ cup)
2 tablespoons soy sauce
2 cups cut-up cooked turkey or chicken
¾ cup seedless grape halves
2 medium stalks celery, thinly sliced
(about 1 cup)
2 green onions, thinly sliced
1 can (11 ounces) mandarin orange
segments, drained
1 can (8 ounces) sliced water
chestnuts, drained

To Complete Recipe:
Lettuce leaves

Mix yogurt and soy sauce in large bowl. Add remaining ingredients except lettuce; toss. See **TO STORE** and **TO SERVE.** *4 servings, about 1½ cups each.*

Per Serving: Calories 255; Protein 24 g; Carbohydrate 30 g (Dietary Fiber 2 g); Fat 5 g (Unsaturated 3 g, Saturated 2 g); Cholesterol 60 mg; Sodium 620 mg. Percent of U.S. RDA: Vitamin A 6%; Vitamin C 20%; Calcium 12%; Iron 12%.

TO STORE

Refrigerator: Cover and refrigerate at least 2 hours until chilled but no longer than 24 hours.

TO SERVE FROM REFRIGERATOR
Serve on lettuce leaves.

Brunch for 8 (page 108)

White Bean Salad

¼ cup olive or vegetable oil
3 tablespoons lemon juice
½ teaspoon pepper
¼ teaspoon salt
¼ cup chopped fresh parsley or 1
tablespoon dried parsley flakes
3 green onions, sliced
1 small red bell pepper, chopped (about ½
cup)
2 cans (15 to 16 ounces each) great
northern beans, drained

To Complete Recipe:
½ cup chopped walnuts

Mix oil, lemon juice, pepper and salt in medium glass or plastic bowl until well blended. Stir in remaining ingredients except walnuts until coated. See **To Store** and **To Serve**. *8 servings, about ½ cup each.*

Per Serving: Calories 215; Protein 9 g; Carbohydrate 23 g (Dietary Fiber 5 g); Fat 12 g (Unsaturated 11 g, Saturated 1 g); Cholesterol 0 mg; Sodium 270 mg. Percent of U.S. RDA: Vitamin A 4%; Vitamin C 6%; Calcium 8%; Iron 18%.

TO STORE

Refrigerator: Cover and refrigerate at least 1 hour but no longer than 5 days.

TO SERVE FROM REFRIGERATOR

Stir in walnuts just before serving.

Piña Colada Mold

1⅔ cups boiling water
2 packages (3 ounces each)
pineapple-orange–flavored gelatin
1 can (6 ounces) frozen piña colada
concentrate
1 can (20 ounces) pineapple tidbits in
juice, drained and juice reserved
½ cup flaked coconut

Pour boiling water on gelatin in medium bowl; stir until gelatin is dissolved. Stir in piña colada concentrate and reserved pineapple juice until concentrate is melted. Refrigerate about 45 minutes or until mixture is consistency of unbeaten egg whites. Stir in pineapple and coconut. Pour into 6-cup mold. See **To Store** and **To Serve**. *8 servings.*

Per Serving: Calories 180; Protein 2 g; Carbohydrate 37 g (Dietary Fiber 1 g); Fat 3 g (Unsaturated 0 g, Saturated 3 g); Cholesterol 0 mg; Sodium 70 mg. Percent of U.S. RDA: Vitamin A *; Vitamin C *; Calcium *; Iron 2%.

TO STORE

Refrigerator: Cover and refregerate at least 4 hours or until set but no longer than 48 hours.

TO SERVE FROM REFRIGERATOR

Unmold onto serving plate lined with salad greens if desired.

Salad Sampler Luncheon for 8 (page 111)

THANK-GOODNESS-IT'S-FRIDAY
GATHERING FOR 10 TO 15

BAKED CHEESE FINGERS*

CREAMY PESTO DIP*

FIVE-SPICE CHICKEN WINGS (SEE PAGE 129)

HERBED CASHEW SNACK MIX (SEE PAGE 139)

Recipe follows

Baked Cheese Fingers

These cheese fingers can be very international! For German flair, stir in ½ cup finely chopped corned beef. For southwest sizzle, substitute 1 tablespoon chopped cilantro for the caraway seed and Monterey Jack cheese for the Swiss cheese.

> *2 egg whites*
> *1 package (3 ounces) cream cheese, softened*
> *¾ teaspoon caraway seed*
> *1 cup shredded Swiss or mozzarella cheese (4 ounces)*
> *1 baguette, 18 inches long (about 8 ounces), cut horizontally in half*

Beat egg whites, cream cheese and caraway seed in small bowl on high speed about 3 minutes or until creamy. Fold in Swiss cheese. Spread cheese mixture onto cut sides of bread. STOP HERE—see **To STORE** and **To COOK.**

To serve now, heat oven to 400°. Place bread halves, cheese sides up, on ungreased cookie sheet. Bake 13 to 15 minutes or until edges are light brown. Cut into 1-inch strips. Serve hot. *About 30 appetizers.*

> **Per Appetizer:** Calories 45; Protein 2 g; Carbohydrate 5 g (Dietary Fiber 0 g); Fat 2 g (Unsaturated 1 g, Saturated 1 g); Cholesterol 10 mg; Sodium 65 mg. Percent of U.S. RDA: Vitamin A *; Vitamin C *; Calcium 4%; Iron 2%.

To STORE
Freezer: Place unbaked bread halves on cookie sheet. Freeze uncovered about 1 hour or until firm. Wrap each half tightly and label. Freeze no longer than 2 months.

To COOK FROM FREEZER
Oven: About 20 minutes before serving, heat oven to 425°. Place bread halves, cheese sides up, on ungreased cookie sheet. Bake 13 to 15 minutes or until edges are light brown. Cut into 1-inch strips. Serve hot.

Creamy Pesto Dip

Surround this pretty dip with an array of fresh vegetables for dipping, such as fresh pea pods, cherry tomatoes and cauliflowerets.

> *½ cup sour cream*
> *½ cup mayonnaise or salad dressing*
> *⅓ cup pesto*
> *2 tablespoons finely sliced green onion*
> *2 teaspoons lemon juice*

To Complete Recipe:
> *Raw vegetables, if desired*

Mix all ingredients except raw vegetables. See **TO STORE** and **TO SERVE**. *1⅓ cups dip.*

Per Tablespoon: Calories 65; Protein 0 g; Carbohydrate 1 g (Dietary Fiber 0 g); Fat 7 g (Unsaturated 5 g, Saturated 2 g); Cholesterol 10 mg; Sodium 55 mg. Percent of U.S. RDA: Vitamin A *; Vitamin C *; Calcium *; Iron *.

TO STORE

Refrigerator: Refrigerate tightly covered at least 1 hour but no longer than 48 hours.

TO SERVE FROM REFRIGERATOR

Serve with raw vegetables.

Baked Pita Chips

> *5 whole wheat pita breads (6 inches in diameter)*

Heat oven to 400°. Cut around outside edges of pita breads to separate layers. Cut each layer into 8 wedges. Place in single layer on 2 ungreased cookie sheets. Bake about 9 minutes or until crisp and light brown; cool. See **TO STORE** and **TO SERVE**. *10 servings, 8 chips each.*

Per Serving: Calories 115; Protein 4g; Carbohydrate 23g (Dietary Fiber 3g); Fat 1g (Unsaturated 1g, Saturated 0g); Cholesterol 0mg; Sodium 240mg. Percent of U.S. RDA: Vitamin A *%; Vitamin C *%; Calcium 2%; Iron 6%.

TO STORE

Freezer: Place in heavy-duty plastic food-storage bag; seal tightly and label. Freeze no longer than 2 months.

TO SERVE FROM FREEZER

About 8 hours before serving, place sealed bag of chips at room temperature to thaw.

4

Raring-to-Go Appetizers

Zesty Italian Dip (page 121); Shrimp-Cheese Bites (page 128)

Havarti Cheese Ball

If you are in a hurry, soften the cream cheese in your microwave. Just remove the foil wrapper and place the cheese in a microwavable bowl. Microwave uncovered on Medium (50%) for 60 to 90 seconds. This is a great recipe to double—serve one right away, and keep the other on hand for impromptu entertaining.

1 package (8 ounces) cream cheese, softened
½ cup shredded Havarti cheese (2 ounces)
⅓ cup crumbled feta cheese (1½ ounces)
2 tablespoons finely chopped green onion
1 tablespoon dry white wine
¾ teaspoon chopped fresh or ¼ teaspoon dried oregano leaves
⅓ cup finely chopped slivered almonds, toasted

To Complete Recipe:
Melba toast rounds, if desired

Beat all ingredients except almonds and toast rounds in medium bowl on low speed until blended. Beat on medium speed, scraping bowl frequently, until fluffy. Cover and refrigerate about 2 hours or until firm enough to shape.

Shape cheese mixture into a ball; roll in almonds. See **To Store** and **To Serve.** *About 1¾ cups spread.*

Per Tablespoon: Calories 45; Protein 1 g; Carbohydrate 1 g (Dietary Fiber 0 g); Fat 4 g (Unsaturated 2 g, Saturated 2 g); Cholesterol 15 mg; Sodium 50 mg. Percent of U.S. RDA: Vitamin A 2%; Vitamin C *; Calcium 2%; Iron *.

To Store

Refrigerator: Refrigerate cheese ball tightly covered at least 2 hours but no longer than 1 week.

Freezer: Wrap cheese ball tightly and label. Freeze no longer than 2 months.

To Serve from Refrigerator

Serve with toast rounds.

To Serve from Freezer

About 1 hour before serving, unwrap cheese ball and let stand at room temperature to thaw. Or thaw loosely wrapped cheese ball in refrigerator at least 8 hours. Serve with toast rounds.

Havarti Cheese Ball; Garlic Olives (page 122)

Pine Nut–Liver Pâté

You'll find this pâté will be soft, even after it's been refrigerated. You can easily double the pâté and store one batch in the freezer.

> *1 tablespoon margarine or butter*
> *¹⁄₂ cup chopped leek*
> *2 cloves garlic, finely chopped*
> *¹⁄₂ pound chicken livers (thawed if frozen)*
> *¹⁄₂ cup chicken broth*
> *³⁄₄ teaspoon fines herbes*
> *¹⁄₄ teaspoon salt*
> *¹⁄₈ teaspoon pepper*
> *¹⁄₄ cup pine nuts*
> *2 tablespoons margarine or butter, softened*

To Complete Recipe:
> *1 tablespoon pine nuts*
> *Cocktail rye bread or crackers, if desired*

Heat 1 tablespoon margarine in 10-inch skillet over medium heat until melted. Cook leek and garlic in margarine about 2 minutes, stirring occasionally, until leek is tender. Stir in chicken livers, broth, fines herbes, salt and pepper; reduce heat. Cover and simmer 12 to 15 minutes or until livers are no longer pink in center. Cool 15 minutes. Drain chicken mixture, reserving ¹⁄₄ cup drippings. (Add water to drippings if necessary to measure ¹⁄₄ cup.)

Place ¹⁄₄ cup pine nuts and 2 tablespoons margarine in blender or food processor. Add chicken mixture and ¹⁄₄ cup drippings. Cover and blend on high speed about 1 minute, stopping blender occasionally to scrape sides, or process 30 seconds, until smooth. Spoon into small crock or bowl. See **To Store** and **To Serve.**
About 1 cup spread.

Microwave: Place 1 tablespoon margarine, the leek and garlic in 1¹⁄₂-quart microwavable casserole. Cover tightly and microwave on High about 2 minutes or until leek is tender. Stir in chicken livers, broth, fines herbes, salt and pepper. Cover tightly and microwave 6 to 7 minutes, stirring after 3 minutes, until chicken is no longer pink in center. Continue as directed above.

Per Tablespoon: Calories 50; Protein 2 g; Carbohydrate 1 g (Dietary Fiber 0 g); Fat 4 g (Unsaturated 3 g, Saturated 1 g); Cholesterol 55 mg; Sodium 90 mg. Percent of U.S. RDA: Vitamin A 44%; Vitamin C *; Calcium *; Iron 4%.

To Store

Refrigerator: Cover pâté tightly and refrigerate at least 4 hours but no longer than 48 hours.

Freezer: Wrap pâté tightly and label. Freeze no longer than 2 months.

To Serve from Refrigerator

Sprinkle with 1 tablespoon pine nuts. Serve with bread.

To Serve from Freezer

About 8 hours before serving, place pâté in refrigerator to thaw. Sprinkle with 1 tablespoon pine nuts. Serve with bread.

Zesty Italian Dip

Tired of the same old celery and carrot sticks? Then perk up your dip with zucchini or jicama strips or fresh mushrooms.

1 cup sour cream
¼ cup finely chopped cucumber
¼ cup thinly sliced green onions (2 to 3 medium)
2 tablespoons milk
1 teaspoon Italian seasoning
⅛ teaspoon salt
⅛ teaspoon ground red pepper (cayenne)
1 clove garlic, finely chopped

To Complete Recipe:
Raw vegetables or bagel chips, if desired

Mix all ingredients except raw vegetables. See **TO STORE** and **TO SERVE.** *About 1½ cups dip.*

Per Tablespoon: Calories 20; Protein 0 g; Carbohydrate 1 g (Dietary Fiber 0 g); Fat 2 g (Unsaturated 1 g, Saturated 1 g); Cholesterol 10 mg; Sodium 15 mg. Percent of U.S. RDA: Vitamin A 2%; Vitamin C *; Calcium *; Iron *.

TO STORE

Refrigerator: Refrigerate tightly covered at least 2 hours but no longer than 24 hours.

TO SERVE FROM REFRIGERATOR

Stir before serving. Serve with raw vegetables.

Smoked Salmon Spread

1 can (14¾ ounces) red salmon, drained and skin and bones removed*
½ package (8-ounce size) cream cheese, softened
½ cup sour cream
¼ cup chopped fresh or 2 tablespoons dried dill weed
1 teaspoon lemon juice
½ teaspoon liquid smoke
2 green onions, chopped

To Complete Recipe:
40 slices cocktail rye or pumpernickel bread
Fresh dill weed, sprigs or chopped

Mix all ingredients except bread and dill weed sprigs. See **TO STORE** and **TO SERVE.** *40 appetizers.*

*1¾ cups flaked smoked salmon can be substituted for the canned salmon and liquid smoke.

Per Tablespoon: Calories 45; Protein 3 g; Carbohydrate 4 g (Dietary Fiber 0 g); Fat 2 g (Unsaturated 1 g, Saturated 1 g); Cholesterol 10 mg; Sodium 115 mg. Percent of U.S. RDA: Vitamin A 2%; Vitamin C *; Calcium 4%; Iron 2%.

TO STORE

Refrigerator: Refrigerate tightly covered at least 2 hours but no longer than 48 hours.

TO SERVE FROM REFRIGERATOR

Spread on bread and top with dill weed.

Zesty Deviled Eggs

6 hard-cooked eggs, peeled
½ cup finely shredded cheese (2 ounces)
2 tablespoons chopped fresh
*   parsley*
3 tablespoons mayonnaise, salad dressing
*   or half-and-half*
1 teaspoon prepared horseradish
½ teaspoon ground mustard
⅛ teaspoon salt
¼ teaspoon pepper
Tiny cooked shrimp, sliced olives,
*   pimiento or parsley, if desired*

Cut eggs lengthwise in half. Slip out yolks and
mash with fork. Stir in remaining ingredients
except shrimp. Fill egg whites with egg yolk
mixture, heaping it lightly. Garnish with shrimp.
See **To Store** and **To Serve.** Can be served
now. *12 appetizers.*

Per Appetizer: Calories 85; Protein 4 g; Carbohydrate 1 g
(Dietary Fiber 0 g); Fat 7 g (Unsaturated 5 g, Saturated 2 g);
Cholesterol 115 mg; Sodium 105 mg. Percent of U.S. RDA:
Vitamin A 4%; Vitamin C *; Calcium 4%; Iron 2%.

To Store

Refrigerator: Refrigerate tightly covered no
longer than 48 hours.

To Serve from Refrigerator

Serve deviled eggs on serving plate lined with
lettuce leaves if desired.

Garlic Olives

1 can (7¾ ounces) unstuffed ripe olives,
*   drained*
1 jar (7 ounces) unstuffed green olives,
*   drained*
¼ cup balsamic, red wine or cider vinegar
½ cup olive or vegetable oil
1 small onion, sliced
2 tablespoons chopped fresh parsley
2 cloves garlic, sliced

Cut each olive halfway around pit, using sharp
knife. Place in glass jar with remaining ingredients. Cover tightly and shake. See **To Store**
and **To Serve.** *About 2 cups olives.*

Per ¼ Cup: Calories 80; Protein 0 g; Carbohydrate
2 g (Dietary Fiber 1 g); Fat 9 g (Unsaturated 8 g, Saturated
1 g); Cholesterol 0 mg; Sodium 600 mg. Percent of U.S.
RDA: Vitamin A*; Vitamin C*; Calcium 2%; Iron 4%.

To Store

Refrigerator: Refrigerate at least 2 hours but
no longer than 1 month.

To Serve from Refrigerator

Drain before serving.

Marinated Mushrooms and Cheese

Marinating is super easy when you use a plastic bag. However, you can also use a covered glass bowl if you like, stirring the mixture occasionally.

½ cup sun-dried tomatoes, cut into bite-size pieces
1 cup boiling water
¼ cup olive or vegetable oil
¼ cup white vinegar
1 tablespoon chopped fresh or 1 teaspoon dried marjoram leaves
1½ teaspoons chopped fresh or ½ teaspoon dried rosemary leaves
¼ teaspoon garlic powder
8 ounces tiny whole mushrooms
8 ounces brick cheese, cut into ½-inch cubes

Mix tomatoes and water. Let stand 5 minutes; drain. Place ½-gallon heavy-duty plastic food-storage bag in bowl. Mix oil, vinegar, marjoram, rosemary and garlic powder in plastic bag. Add tomatoes, mushrooms and cheese to bag; seal tightly. See **TO STORE** and **TO SERVE.** *12 servings, about ¼ cup each.*

Per Serving: Calories 90; Protein 5 g; Carbohydrate 2 g (Dietary Fiber 0 g); Fat 7 g (Unsaturated 3 g, Saturated 4 g); Cholesterol 20 mg; Sodium 190 mg. Percent of U.S. RDA: Vitamin A 6%; Vitamin C *; Calcium 14%; Iron 2%.

TO STORE

Refrigerator: Refrigerate at least 4 hours but no longer than 4 days, turning occasionally.

TO SERVE FROM REFRIGERATOR

Drain before serving.

Turkey-stuffed Mushrooms

For a spicier appetizer, make these savory morsels with bulk turkey sausage rather than ground turkey.

36 medium mushrooms (about 1 pound)
6 ounces ground turkey
¼ cup shredded carrot
¼ cup finely chopped apple
1 cup soft bread crumbs (about 1½ slices bread)
½ teaspoon poultry seasoning
½ teaspoon onion powder
¼ teaspoon pepper

Remove stems from mushrooms. Finely chop enough stems to measure ⅓ cup. Cook mushroom stems, ground turkey, carrot and apple in 10-inch skillet over medium heat about 4 minutes, stirring frequently, until turkey is no longer pink; remove from heat. Stir in remaining ingredients. Fill mushroom caps with turkey mixture. STOP HERE—see **To Store** and **To Cook.**

To serve now, heat oven to 400°. Grease rectangular pan, 13 × 9 × 2 inches. Place mushroom caps, filled sides up, evenly in pan. Bake uncovered 12 to 14 minutes or until filling is hot. Serve hot. *36 appetizers.*

Microwave: Arrange mushroom caps, filled sides up (smallest mushrooms in center), on two 10-inch microwavable plates. Microwave 1 plate at a time uncovered on High 1½ to 2 minutes, rotating plate ½ turn after 1 minute, until filling is hot.

Per Appetizer: Calories 25; Protein 1 g; Carbohydrate 3 g (Dietary Fiber 0 g); Fat 1 g (Unsaturated 1 g, Saturated 0 g); Cholesterol 5 mg; Sodium 25 mg. Percent of U.S. RDA: Vitamin A 2%; Vitamin C *; Calcium *; Iron 2%.

To Store

Refrigerator: Refrigerate uncooked filled mushroom caps tightly covered no longer than 24 hours.

Freezer: Place uncooked filled mushroom caps in single layer in labeled airtight freezer container. Freeze no longer than 2 months.

To Cook from Refrigerator

Oven: About 25 minutes before serving, heat oven to 400°. Grease rectangular pan, 13 × 9 × 2 inches. Place mushroom caps, filled sides up, evenly in pan. Bake uncovered 14 to 16 minutes or until filling is hot. Serve hot.

Microwave: Arrange refrigerated mushroom caps, filled sides up (smallest mushrooms in center), on two 10-inch microwavable plates. Microwave 1 plate at a time uncovered on High 2 to 3 minutes, rotating plate ½ turn after 1 minute, until hot. Serve hot.

To Cook from Freezer

Oven: About 30 minutes before serving, heat oven to 400°. Grease rectangular pan, 13 × 9 × 2 inches. Place mushroom caps, filled sides up, evenly in pan. Bake uncovered 15 to 17 minutes or until filling is hot.

Cheese-filled Triangles

1 pound feta cheese*
2 eggs, slightly beaten
2 tablespoons chopped fresh or 2
    teaspoons dried basil leaves
2 tablespoons chopped fresh or 2
    teaspoons dried oregano leaves
¼ teaspoon white pepper
1 package (16 ounces) frozen phyllo
    sheets (18 × 14 inches), thawed
⅓ cup margarine or butter, melted

Grease cookie sheet. Crumble cheese into small bowl; mash with fork. Stir in eggs, basil, oregano and white pepper until well mixed. Cut phyllo sheets lengthwise into 2-inch strips. Cover with plastic wrap, then with damp towel to keep them from drying out. Place 1 level teaspoon cheese mixture on end of 1 strip. Fold strip over cheese mixture end over end in triangular shape to opposite end. Place on cookie sheet. Repeat with remaining strips and cheese mixture. Brush triangles lightly with margarine. STOP HERE—**To Store** and **To Cook.**

To serve now, heat oven to 400°. Bake 12 to 15 minutes or until puffed and golden brown. *72 appetizers.*

*Finely shredded Monterey Jack cheese can be substituted for the feta cheese.

Per Appetizer: Calories 40; Protein 1 g; Carbohydrate 4 g (Dietary Fiber 0 g); Fat 2 g (Unsaturated 1 g, Saturated 1 g); Cholesterol 10 mg; Sodium 105 mg. Percent of U.S. RDA: Vitamin A 2%; Vitamin C *; Calcium 2%; Iron 2%.

To Store

Refrigerator: Cover unbaked triangles tightly and refrigerate no longer than 24 hours.

Freezer: Cool triangles on wire rack. Freeze uncovered on ungreased cookie sheet at least 2 hours until firm. Place in heavy-duty plastic food-storage bag; seal tightly and label. Freeze no longer than 2 months.

To Cook from Refrigerator

Oven: About 30 minutes before serving, heat oven to 400°. Bake about 15 minutes or until puffed and golden.

To Cook from Freezer

Oven: About 30 minutes before serving, heat oven to 375°. Place triangles on ungreased cookie sheet. Bake 15 to 20 minutes or until puffed and golden.

Note: Triangles can be baked before freezing. Follow baking instructions for baking "to serve now." About 20 minutes before serving baked triangles from the freezer, heat oven to 350°. Place triangles on ungreased cookie sheet. Bake 7 to 8 minutes or until hot.

Reuben Mini-Stacks

¾ cup shredded Swiss cheese (3 ounces)
6 thin slices corned beef (1 ounce), finely chopped
3 tablespoons Thousand Island dressing
2 tablespoons finely chopped drained sauerkraut
12 slices cocktail rye or pumpernickel bread

To Complete Recipe:
12 tiny dill pickles, cut lengthwise in half

Mix cheese, corned beef, dressing and sauerkraut. Spread over each slice bread, covering to edges. STOP HERE—see **To Store** and **To Cook.**

To complete recipe and serve now, set oven control to broil. Place topped bread on rack in broiler pan or on ungreased cookie sheet. Broil with tops 4 to 5 inches from heat 2 to 3 minutes or until golden. Top each with 2 pickle halves. *12 appetizers.*

Per Appetizer: Calories 70; Protein 3 g; Carbohydrate 6 g (Dietary Fiber 1 g); Fat 4 g (Unsaturated 2 g, Saturated 2 g); Cholesterol 10 mg; Sodium 620 mg. Percent of U.S. RDA: Vitamin A 2%; Vitamin C *; Calcium 8%; Iron 2%.

TO STORE

Freezer: Place topped bread in single layer in labeled airtight freezer container. Freeze no longer than 2 months.

TO COOK FROM FREEZER

Broiler: About 20 minutes before serving, set oven control to broil. Place topped bread on rack in broiler pan or on ungreased cookie sheet. Broil with tops 5 to 6 inches from heat 5 to 6 minutes or until golden. Top each with 2 pickle halves.

To Do Ahead

✓ Havarti cheese Ball

✓ Garlic Olives

Reuben mini-Stacks

Shrimp-Cheese Bites

½ cup (1 stick) margarine or butter
1¼ cups all-purpose flour
1 egg, beaten
⅔ cup chopped cooked shrimp
2 ounces farmer or goat cheese, crumbled
1 egg
1 egg yolk
½ cup half-and-half
2 teaspoons chopped fresh or ¾ teaspoon
  dried basil leaves

Heat oven to 375°. Cut margarine into flour with pastry blender or two knives in medium bowl until mixture is crumbly. Stir in 1 beaten egg until well mixed; shape into ball. Divide into 24 balls. Press 1 ball on bottom and up side of each of 24 ungreased small muffin cups, 1¼ × 1 inch. Divide shrimp among cups. Sprinkle with cheese. Beat 1 egg and the egg yolk in small bowl; stir in half-and-half and basil. Spoon about 1 tablespoon egg mixture into each cup. Bake about 20 minutes or until light brown. Immediately remove from pans to wire rack. STOP HERE—see **TO STORE** and **TO REHEAT.** Can be served now. *24 appetizers.*

Per Appetizer: Calories 85; Protein 3 g; Carbohydrate 5 g (Dietary Fiber 0 g); Fat 6 g (Unsaturated 4 g, Saturated 2 g); Cholesterol 45 mg; Sodium 80 mg. Percent of U.S. RDA: Vitamin A 8%; Vitamin C *; Calcium 2%; Iron 2%.

TO STORE

Refrigerator: Cool bites completely on wire rack. Refrigerate tightly covered no longer than 24 hours.

Freezer: Cool bites completely on wire rack. Place in single layer on cookie sheet. Freeze uncovered at least 2 hours. Place bites in labeled airtight freezer container. Freeze no longer than 2 months.

TO REHEAT FROM REFRIGERATOR

Oven: About 25 minutes before serving, heat oven to 350°. Bake on ungreased cookie sheet about 15 minutes or until warm.

TO REHEAT FROM FREEZER

Oven: About 30 minutes before serving, heat oven to 350°. Bake on ungreased cookie sheet about 18 minutes or until warm.

Five-Spice Chicken Wings

You can make a tasty main dish with the same delightful spicing as these chicken wings. Just substitute 1½ pounds chicken pieces for the wings, and cut the rest of the ingredients in half. Continue as directed below—except bake in a 9 × 9 × 2-inch pan.

3½ pounds chicken wings (about 20)
¼ cup soy sauce
¼ cup honey
2 tablespoons chili puree with
    garlic or 2 tablespoons chili sauce plus
    2 cloves garlic, finely chopped
1 tablespoon vegetable oil
½ teaspoon five-spice powder
½ teaspoon finely chopped gingerroot or
    ¼ teaspoon ground ginger
½ teaspoon sesame oil

Cut each chicken wing at joints to make 3 pieces; discard tip. Mix remaining ingredients in 1-gallon heavy-duty plastic food-storage bag. Add chicken; seal bag tightly. (If planning to microwave, use covered rectangular microwavable dish, 11 × 7 × 1½ inches.) Refrigerate at least 1 hour but no longer than 24 hours, turning occasionally.

Heat oven to 375°. Line broiler pan with aluminum foil. Remove chicken from marinade; reserve marinade. Place chicken on rack in broiler pan.

Bake uncovered 25 minutes. Brush with marinade; turn. Bake about 25 minutes longer, brushing occasionally with marinade, until juice of chicken is no longer pink when centers of thickest pieces are cut. Discard any remaining marinade. STOP HERE—see **To Store** and **To Reheat.** Can be served now. *About 20 appetizers.*

Microwave: Drain chicken and discard marinade. Cover dish with plastic wrap, folding back 1 corner to vent. Microwave on High 12 to 15 minutes, rotating dish ½ turn after 6 minutes, until juice of chicken is no longer pink when centers of thickest pieces are cut.

Per Appetizer: Calories 85; Protein 7 g; Carbohydrate 1 g (Dietary Fiber 0 g); Fat 6 g (Unsaturated 4 g, Saturated 2 g); Cholesterol 25 mg; Sodium 80 mg. Percent of U.S. RDA: Vitamin A 2%; Vitamin C *; Calcium *; Iron 2%.

To Store

Refrigerator: Cover baked chicken tightly and refrigerate no longer than 4 days.

Freezer: Place baked chicken in labeled airtight freezer container. Freeze no longer than 3 weeks.

To Reheat from Freezer

Oven: About 20 minutes before serving, heat oven to 375°. Line broiler pan with aluminum foil. Place chicken in single layer on rack in broiler pan. Bake uncovered 8 to 10 minutes or until hot.

To Reheat from Freezer

Oven: About 15 minutes before serving, heat oven to 375°. Cover cookie sheet with aluminum foil. Bake chicken in single layer on foil about 10 minutes or until hot.

Microwave: Place frozen chicken in rectangular microwavable dish, 11 × 7 × 1½ inches. Cover loosely and microwave on High 8 to 10 minutes, rearranging chicken after 4 minutes, until hot.

Savory Chicken Cheesecake

This delicious cheesecake can also be served as a spread. Divide the cream cheese mixture among six lightly greased 10-ounce soufflé dishes. Bake at 300° about 40 minutes or until set in center—the edges will not be brown. Refrigerate or freeze as instructed. You can top each dish with a different condiment, such as chutney, cranberry sauce, pesto or apple butter. Serve with sturdy crackers.

> 2 packages (8 ounces each) cream
>   cheese, softened
> 1 container (8 ounces) sour cream–and-
>   onion dip
> 1 tablespoon all-purpose flour
> 1½ teaspoons chopped fresh or ½ tea-
>   spoon dried dill weed
> 3 eggs
> 1 cup finely chopped cooked
>   chicken or smoked turkey

To Complete Recipe:
> ½ cup cranberry-orange relish, drained,
>   or chutney
> 2 tablespoons chopped walnuts, toasted

Heat oven to 300°. Lightly grease springform pan, 8 × 3 inches. Beat cream cheese in medium bowl on medium speed until fluffy. Beat in dip, flour and dill weed. Beat in eggs, one at a time.

Fold in chicken. Spread in pan. Bake about 1¼ hours or until edge is golden brown and center is firm. Cool 15 minutes. Run metal spatula along side of cheesecake to loosen. STOP HERE—see **To Store** and **To Serve**. *16 to 24 servings.*

Per Serving: Calories 175; Protein 6 g; Carbohydrate 6 g (Dietary Fiber 0 g); Fat 14 g (Unsaturated 6 g, Saturated 8 g); Cholesterol 90 mg; Sodium 210 mg. Percent of U.S. RDA: Vitamin A 10%; Vitamin C *; Calcium 4%; Iron 4%.

TO STORE

Refrigerator: Cover tightly and refrigerate at least 4 hours but no longer than 24 hours.

Freezer: *Do not refrigerate cheesecake.* Wrap cheesecake and pan tightly and label. Freeze no longer than 1 month.

TO SERVE FROM REFRIGERATOR

Run metal spatula along sides of cheesecake to loosen. Remove side of pan. Spoon relish onto center of cheesecake (if using chutney, chop large pieces). Sprinkle with walnuts. Cut into slices.

TO SERVE FROM FREEZER

About 24 hours before serving, place cheesecake in refrigerator to thaw. Run metal spatula along side of cheesecake to loosen. Remove side of pan. Spoon relish onto center of cheesecake (if using chutney, chop large pieces). Sprinkle with walnuts. Cut into slices.

Savory Chicken Cheesecake

Apricot-Pork Meatballs

¾ pound ground pork or beef
⅓ cup dry bread crumbs
¼ cup finely chopped dried apricots
1 teaspoon soy sauce
½ teaspoon five-spice powder
¼ teaspoon garlic powder
1 egg

To Complete Recipe:
Spicy Apricot Glaze (right)

Heat oven to 350°. Mix all ingredients except Spicy Apricot Glaze. Shape mixture into 20 meatballs. Place in ungreased rectangular pan, 13 × 9 × 2 inches. Bake uncovered about 20 minutes or until no longer pink in center; drain well. STOP HERE—see **To Store** and **To Reheat**. *20 appetizers.*

To serve now, prepare Spicy Apricot Glaze. Serve with meatballs.

Microwave: Mix all ingredients except Spicy Apricot Glaze. Shape mixture into 20 meatballs. Place in rectangular microwavable dish, 11 × 7 × 1½ inches. Cover with waxed paper and microwave on High 6 to 8 minutes, rearranging meatballs after 3 minutes, until no longer pink in center. Let stand covered 3 minutes; drain.

For glaze, mix all ingredients in small microwavable bowl. Cover tightly and microwave on High 1 to 2 minutes, stirring every minute, until hot.

SPICY APRICOT GLAZE

½ cup apricot preserves
⅓ cup stir-fry or sweet-and-sour sauce
¼ teaspoon five-spice powder

Mix all ingredients in 1-quart saucepan. Heat over medium heat, stirring occasionally, until sauce is hot.

> **Per Appetizer:** Calories 90; Protein 4 g; Carbohydrate 9 g (Dietary Fiber 0 g); Fat 4 g (Unsaturated 3 g, Saturated 1 g); Cholesterol 20 mg; Sodium 55 mg. Percent of U.S. RDA: Vitamin A 2%; Vitamin C *; Calcium *; Iron 2%.

TO STORE

Freezer: Place drained cooked meatballs in single layer on cookie sheet. Freeze uncovered about 1 hour or until firm. Place meatballs in labeled airtight freezer container. Freeze no longer than 2 months.

TO REHEAT FROM FREEZER

Oven: About 30 minutes before serving, heat oven to 400°. Place meatballs in single layer in ungreased rectangular pan, 13 × 9 × 2 inches. Bake uncovered 15 to 20 minutes or until hot. Prepare Spicy Apricot Glaze. Serve with meatballs.

Microwave: About 10 minutes before serving, place frozen meatballs on large 10-inch microwavable plate. Cover with plastic wrap, folding back about 2 inches at edge to vent. Microwave on Medium (50%) 5 to 6 minutes, rearranging meatballs after 3 minutes, until hot. Prepare Spicy Apricot Glaze. Serve with meatballs.

Apricot-Pork Meatballs

Cranberry Barbecued Ribs

This savory cranberry glaze is also delicious brushed over chicken wings or drummies. Try it with appetizer meatballs too!

> *3 pounds fresh pork riblets or 3-pound*
> *rack back ribs, cut lengthwise across*
> *bones in half*
> *1 cup whole berry cranberry sauce*
> *½ cup hoisin sauce*
> *½ teaspoon onion powder*
> *¼ teaspoon salt*
> *⅛ teaspoon pepper*

Heat oven to 375°. Grease broiler pan rack. Trim fat and remove membranes from pork riblets. (For ribs, cut between bones into serving pieces.) Place pork, meaty sides up, in single layer on rack in broiler pan. Cover with aluminum foil and bake 50 minutes. Mix remaining ingredients. Brush pork with half of the cranberry mixture. Bake uncovered 10 to 20 minutes longer or until pork is tender. STOP HERE— see **To Store** and **To Reheat.**

To serve now, heat remaining cranberry mixture to boiling in 1-quart saucepan. Serve with pork. *About 40 appetizers.*

Per Appetizer: Calories 60; Protein 3 g; Carbohydrate 3 g (Dietary Fiber 0 g); Fat 4 g (Unsaturated 3 g, Saturated 1 g); Cholesterol 10 mg; Sodium 160 mg. Percent of U.S. RDA: Vitamin A *; Vitamin C *; Calcium *; Iron *.

To Store

Refrigerator: Place cooked pork in rectangular glass baking dish, 13 × 9 × 2 inches; cover tightly with aluminum foil. Refrigerate remaining cranberry mixture in tightly covered container. Refrigerate pork and cranberry mixture no longer than 48 hours.

To Reheat from Refrigerator

Oven: About 35 minutes before serving, heat oven to 400°. Bake pork in covered dish about 20 minutes or until hot. Heat remaining cranberry mixture to boiling in 1-quart saucepan. Serve with pork.

Cranberry Barbecued Ribs

Appetizer Chicken Puffs

Unfilled, these puffs freeze well. Place them in a freezer bag, seal, label and freeze no longer than 2 months. To serve, thaw at room temperature about 30 minutes.

½ cup water
¼ cup (½ stick) margarine or butter
½ cup all-purpose flour
1½ teaspoons chopped fresh or ½ tea-
*   spoon dried thyme leaves*
2 eggs
1 cup chopped cooked chicken
⅓ cup finely chopped green bell pepper
½ cup Caesar dressing
2 tablespoons sunflower nuts
2 tablespoons grated Parmesan cheese

To Complete Recipe:
*   3 cherry tomatoes, cut into fourths*

Heat oven to 400°. Heat water and margarine to rolling boil in 2-quart saucepan. Stir in flour and thyme; reduce heat. Stir vigorously over low heat about 1 minute or until mixture forms a ball; remove from heat. Beat in eggs, one at a time, beating until smooth after each addition. Drop dough by heaping teaspoonfuls about 2 inches apart onto ungreased cookie sheet.

Bake 25 to 30 minutes or until puffed and golden brown. Cool on cookie sheet away from draft. Cut off top one-third of each puff and pull out any filaments of soft dough. Mix remaining ingredients except tomatoes. STOP HERE— see **To Store** and **To Serve.**

To complete recipe and serve now, fill each bottom of puff with 1 rounded tablespoon chicken mixture. Top with cherry tomato fourth; replace top. *12 appetizers.*

Per Appetizer: Calories 155; Protein 6 g; Carbohydrate 6 g (Dietary Fiber 0 g); Fat 12 g (Unsaturated 10 g, Saturated 2 g); Cholesterol 45 mg; Sodium 200 mg. Percent of U.S. RDA: Vitamin A 6%; Vitamin C *; Calcium 2%; Iron 4%.

To Store

Refrigerator: Cover chicken mixture tightly and refrigerate no longer than 24 hours. Cover puffs loosely and store in single layer at room temperature no longer than 48 hours.

To Serve from Refrigerator

Fill each bottom of puff with 1 rounded table-spoon chicken mixture. Top with cherry tomato fourth; replace top.

Mexican Meatballs

2 jalapeño chilies
1 pound ground beef
½ cup dry bread crumbs
¼ cup shredded Monterey Jack or
*   Cheddar cheese (1 ounce)*
¼ cup milk
1 teaspoon salt
¼ teaspoon pepper
1 egg
1 small onion, finely chopped (about
*   ¼ cup)*
2 cups salsa

Heat oven to 400°. Remove stems, seeds and membranes from chilies; chop chilies. Mix chilies and remaining ingredients except salsa. Shape mixture into 1-inch balls. Place in ungreased rectangular pan, 13 × 9 × 2 inches. Bake uncovered 15 to 20 minutes or until no longer pink in center. STOP HERE—See **To Store** and **To Reheat.**

To serve now, place meatballs in 2-quart saucepan; add salsa. Heat over medium heat, stirring occasionally, until hot. Place meatballs in chafing dish. *12 servings, 3 meatballs each.*

Per Serving: Calories 125; Protein 10g; Carbohydrate 7g (Dietary Fiber 1g); Fat 7g (Unsaturated 4g, Saturated 3g); Cholesterol 40mg; Sodium 530mg. Percent of U.S. RDA: Vitamin A 32%; Vitamin C 24%; Calcium 4%; Iron 6%.

To Store

Freezer: Place meatballs in labeled airtight 2-quart freezer container. Pour salsa over meatballs. Cover and freeze no longer than 2 months.

To Reheat from Freezer

Stovetop: About 24 hours before serving, place meatballs in refrigerator to thaw. Dip container into hot water to loosen; remove container. Heat meatballs in 2-quart saucepan over medium heat, stirring occasionally, until hot. Place meatballs in chafing dish.

Herbed Whole Wheat Breadsticks

1 package regular active dry yeast
1 cup warm water (105° to 115°)
2 cups all-purpose flour
2 tablespoons vegetable oil
1½ tablespoons chopped fresh or 1½
*   teaspoons dried basil leaves*
1 tablespoon chopped fresh or 1 teaspoon
*   dried tarragon leaves*
1 teaspoon salt
1 to 1½ cups whole wheat flour
Cornmeal
1 egg white
2 tablespoons cold water
Sesame seed, toasted

Dissolve yeast in warm water in large bowl. Stir in all-purpose flour, oil, basil, tarragon and salt. Stir in enough whole wheat flour to make dough easy to handle (dough will be soft). Turn dough onto surface lightly sprinkled with whole wheat flour; gently roll in flour to coat. Knead about 5 minutes or until smooth and elastic. Place dough in greased medium bowl and turn greased side up. Cover and let rise in warm place 1 to 1½ hours or until double.

Grease 2 cookie sheets; sprinkle with cornmeal. Punch down dough. Divide into 24 equal parts. Roll and shape each part into rope, about 8 inches long, sprinkling with whole wheat flour if dough is too sticky. Place on cookie sheet. Cover and let rise in warm place 30 to 40 minutes or until double.

Heat oven to 400°. Mix egg white and cold water; brush over breadsticks. Sprinkle with sesame seed. Bake about 15 minutes or until golden brown. Immediately remove from cookie sheets to wire rack. STOP HERE—see **To Store** and **To Serve**.

Can be served now, hot or cool. *24 breadsticks.*

> **Per Breadstick:** Calories 70; Protein 2 g; Carbohydrate 12 g (Dietary Fiber 1 g); Fat 2 g (Unsaturated 2 g, Saturated 0 g); Cholesterol 0 mg; Sodium 95 mg. Percent of U.S. RDA: Vitamin A *; Vitamin C *; Calcium *; Iron 4%.

TO STORE

Freezer: Place cooled breadsticks in heavy-duty plastic food-storage bag; seal tightly and label. Freeze no longer than 2 months.

TO SERVE FROM FREEZER

About 10 minutes before serving, unwrap breadsticks and let stand at room temperature to thaw.

Herbed Cashew Snack Mix

Keep them guessing by making this snack mix with different nuts and spices, such as pecans and basil.

> *2 cups bite-size squares oven-*
>   *toasted corn cereal*
> *2 cups bite-size shredded wheat cereal*
> *2 cups pretzel stick*
> *1 cup cashews*
> *¼ cup (½ stick) margarine or butter*
> *1½ teaspoons chopped fresh or ½*
>   *teaspoon dried tarragon leaves*
> *1 teaspoon onion powder*
> *¼ teaspoon red pepper sauce*

Heat oven to 325°. Mix cereals, pretzel sticks and cashews in ungreased rectangular pan, 13 × 9 × 2 inches. Heat margarine in 1-quart saucepan until melted; remove from heat. Stir in remaining ingredients. Pour over cereal mixture, tossing until thoroughly coated. Bake uncovered about 25 minutes, stirring occasionally, until hot. STOP HERE—see **To Store** and **To Serve.**

To serve now, cool slightly. Serve warm or cool. *About 6 cups snack mix.*

Microwave: Mix cereals, pretzel sticks and cashews in 4-quart microwavable bowl. Place margarine in 1-cup microwavable measure. Microwave margarine uncovered on High about 30 seconds or until melted. Stir in remaining ingredients. Pour over cereal mixture, tossing until thoroughly coated. Microwave cereal mixture uncovered on High 4 to 5 minutes, stirring every 2 minutes, until hot. Serve warm or cool.

> **Per ½ Cup:** Calories 165; Protein 3 g; Carbohydrate 18 g (Dietary Fiber 2 g); Fat 10 g (Unsaturated 8 g, Saturated 2 g); Cholesterol 0 mg; Sodium 280 mg. Percent of U.S. RDA: Vitamin A 4%; Vitamin C *; Calcium *%; Iron 12%.

To Store

Refrigerator: Cool snack mix. Refrigerate tightly covered no longer than 1 week.

Freezer: Cool snack mix. Place in labeled airtight freezer container. Freeze no longer than 2 weeks.

To Serve from Freezer

About 30 minutes before serving, uncover snack mix and let stand at room temperature to thaw.

5

Made-in-Advance
Delectable Desserts

Italian Pistachio Torte (page 143)

Cappuccino Cake Roll

3 eggs
1 cup granulated sugar
¼ cup cold espresso or double-strength coffee
2 tablespoons coffee liqueur, cold espresso or double-strength coffee
1 teaspoon vanilla
½ cup all-purpose flour
¼ cup whole wheat flour
1 teaspoon baking powder
¼ teaspoon ground cinnamon
1 cup whipping (heavy) cream
3 tablespoons coffee liqueur*

To Complete Recipe:
Powdered sugar

Heat oven to 375°. Line jelly roll pan, 15½ × 10½ × 1 inch, with cooking parchment paper, aluminum foil or waxed paper. Generously grease paper or foil. Beat eggs in small bowl on high speed about 5 minutes or until very thick and lemon colored. Pour eggs into medium bowl. Gradually beat in granulated sugar. Beat in espresso, 2 tablespoons liqueur and the vanilla on low speed. Gradually add flours, baking powder and cinnamon to egg mixture, beating just until batter is smooth. Pour into pan, spreading to corners.

Bake 12 to 15 minutes or until toothpick inserted in center comes out clean. Immediately loosen cake from edges of pan and invert onto towel generously sprinkled with powdered sugar. Carefully remove paper or foil. Trim off stiff edges of cake if necessary. While hot, carefully roll cake and towel from narrow end. Cool on wire rack at least 30 minutes.

Beat whipping cream and 3 tablespoons liqueur in chilled medium bowl until stiff. Unroll cake and remove towel. Spread whipped cream over cake. Roll up cake. See **TO STORE** and **TO SERVE**. *10 servings.*

*3 tablespoons espresso or double-strength coffee and 3 tablespoons powdered sugar can be substituted for the coffee liqueur.

Per Serving: Calories 225; Protein 3 g; Carbohydrate 31 g (Dietary Fiber 0 g); Fat 10 g (Unsaturated 4 g, Saturated 6 g); Cholesterol 95 mg; Sodium 65 mg. Percent of U.S. RDA: Vitamin A 10%; Vitamin C *; Calcium 4%; Iron 4%.

TO STORE

Refrigerator: Refrigerate cake roll tightly covered at least 2 hours but no longer than 48 hours.

Freezer: Wrap cake roll tightly and label. Freeze at least 12 hours but no longer than 1 month.

TO SERVE FROM REFRIGERATOR
Sprinkle with powdered sugar.

TO SERVE FROM FREEZER

About 15 minutes before serving, unwrap and place on serving plate. Let stand at room temperature 10 minutes before cutting. Sprinkle with powdered sugar.

Italian Pistachio Torte

This elegant torte features the creamy filling usually found in cannoli pastries, spread between luscious layers of pistachio pound cake.

1⅔ cups granulated sugar
¾ cup (1½ sticks) margarine or butter, softened
1 teaspoon vanilla
3 eggs
1¾ cups all-purpose flour
¾ teaspoon baking powder
⅔ cup milk
½ cup chopped dry-roasted or toasted pistachio nuts
1½ cups ricotta cheese
¾ cup powdered sugar
⅓ cup miniature semisweet chocolate chips
3 tablespoons milk
1½ teaspoons vanilla
¼ cup miniature semisweet chocolate chips
1 tablespoon margarine or butter
1 tablespoon corn syrup
1 teaspoon hot water

Heat oven to 325°. Grease and flour loaf pan, 9 × 5 × 3 inches. Beat granulated sugar, ¾ cup margarine, 1 teaspoon vanilla and the eggs in large bowl on low speed 30 seconds, scraping bowl constantly. Beat on high speed 5 minutes, scraping bowl occasionally. Beat in flour and baking powder alternately with ⅔ cup milk on low speed. Fold ⅓ cup of the pistachio nuts into batter. Spread batter in pan.

Bake 1 hour 5 minutes to 1 hour 15 minutes or until toothpick inserted in center comes out clean. Cool 20 minutes; remove from pan. Cool completely on wire rack. Split cake horizontally to make 3 layers. (To split, mark sides of cake with toothpicks and cut with long, thin serrated knife.)

Mix ricotta cheese, powdered sugar, ⅓ cup chocolate chips, 3 tablespoons milk and 1½ teaspoons vanilla. Spread ricotta mixture over bottom and middle cake layers; stack layers. Add top cake layer.

Heat ¼ cup chocolate chips, 1 tablespoon margarine and the corn syrup in 1-quart saucepan over low heat, stirring constantly, until chocolate is melted; cool slightly. Stir in water. Spread chocolate mixture over top of torte. Sprinkle with remaining pistachio nuts. Let stand until chocolate mixture is firm. See **TO STORE** and **TO SERVE.** *10 servings.*

Per Serving: Calories 560; Protein 11 g; Carbohydrate 72 g (Dietary Fiber 2 g); Fat 26 g (Unsaturated 18 g, Saturated 8 g); Cholesterol 75 mg; Sodium 280 mg. Percent of U.S. RDA: Vitamin A 28%; Vitamin C *; Calcium 16%; Iron 12%.

TO STORE

Refrigerator: Refrigerate torte tightly covered at least 2 hours but no longer than 48 hours.

Freezer: Wrap torte tightly and label. Freeze no longer than 1 month.

TO SERVE FROM REFRIGERATOR

Use sharp knife to slice.

TO SERVE FROM FREEZER

About 1 hour before serving, unwrap torte and place on serving plate. Let stand at room temperature to thaw. Use sharp knife to slice.

Chocolate Dream Tart

⅓ cup margarine or butter, softened
1 cup all-purpose flour
1 egg
1 tablespoon margarine or butter
1 can (14 ounces) sweetened
   condensed milk
1 package (12 ounces) semisweet
   chocolate chips (2 cups)
½ cup chopped walnuts
1 teaspoon vanilla

To Complete Recipe:
   Unsweetened whipped cream, if desired
   8 to 10 walnut halves, toasted, if desired

Heat oven to 400°. Cut ⅓ cup margarine into flour until mixture is crumbly. Mix in egg until dough forms. Shape dough into a ball. Press firmly and evenly against bottom and side of ungreased tart pan, 9 × 1 inch. Bake 10 to 12 minutes or until light brown; cool.

Reduce oven temperature to 350°. Heat 1 tablespoon margarine in 2-quart saucepan until melted. Stir in milk and chocolate chips. Cook over low heat, stirring occasionally, until chocolate is melted. Stir in chopped walnuts and vanilla. Spread in baked crust. Bake about 25 minutes or until edge is set but chocolate appears moist in center. Cool in pan on wire rack. STOP HERE—see **To Store** and **To Serve.**

To serve now, top each slice with whipped cream and walnut half. *8 to 10 servings.*

Per Serving: Calories 570; Protein 9 g; Carbohydrate 68 g (Dietary Fiber 4 g); Fat 31 g (Unsaturated 18 g, Saturated 13 g); Cholesterol 45 mg; Sodium 180 mg. Percent of U.S. RDA: Vitamin A 16%; Vitamin C *; Calcium 16%; Iron 12%.

TO STORE

Refrigerator: Cover cooled tart tightly and refrigerate no longer than 3 days.

Freezer: Wrap cooled tart tightly and label. Freeze no longer than 2 months.

TO SERVE FROM REFRIGERATOR

Top each slice with whipped cream and walnut half.

TO SERVE FROM FREEZER

About 1 hour before serving, unwrap and let stand at room temperature to thaw. Top each slice with whipped cream and walnut half.

Apple Pie

If you like your pie sweeter, use the larger amount of sugar listed. This is a great recipe to double, as it's always handy to have an apple pie ready and waiting in the freezer!

*Pastry for 9-inch Two-Crust Pie
   (see page 149)*
⅓ to ⅔ cup sugar
¼ cup all-purpose flour
½ teaspoon ground nutmeg
½ teaspoon ground cinnamon
Dash of salt
*8 cups thinly sliced peeled tart apples
   (about 8 medium)*
2 tablespoons margarine or butter

To Complete Recipe:
   Ice cream, if desired
   *Caramel or caramel-fudge ice-cream
      topping, if desired*

Heat oven to 425°. Prepare pastry. Mix sugar, flour, nutmeg, cinnamon and salt in large bowl. Stir in apples. Turn into pastry-lined pie plate. Dot with margarine. Cover with top crust that has slits cut in it; seal securely and flute. Cover edge with 3-inch strip of aluminum foil to prevent excessive browning. Remove foil during last 15 minutes of baking. Bake 40 to 50 minutes or until crust is brown and juice begins to bubble through slits in crust. STOP HERE—see **TO STORE** and **TO REHEAT.**

To complete recipe and serve now, cool slightly on wire rack. Serve warm or cold with ice cream and caramel topping. Store loosely covered at room temperature no longer than 3 days. Refrigerate in humid weather. *8 servings.*

Per Serving: Calories 355; Protein 2 g; Carbohydrate 40 g (Dietary Fiber 3 g); Fat 22 g (Unsaturated 17 g, Saturated 5 g); Cholesterol 0 mg; Sodium 135 mg. Percent of U.S. RDA: Vitamin A 4%; Vitamin C *; Calcium *; Iron 6%.

TO STORE

Freezer: Cool baked pie on wire rack about 2 hours or until barely warm. Freeze uncovered at least 3 hours until completely frozen. Wrap tightly and label. Freeze no longer than 4 months.

TO REHEAT FROM FREEZER

About 1¼ hours before serving, unwrap pie and let stand at room temperature 1 hour to thaw. (Place in pie plate if pie was removed from pie plate before freezing.) Move oven rack to lowest position. Heat oven to 375°. Bake 35 to 40 minutes or until warm. Serve warm or cold with ice cream and caramel topping.

Note: If you prefer, line pie plate before preparing and baking with heavy-duty aluminum foil circle cut 3 inches larger than inverted pie plate. After pie is frozen at least 6 hours, remove pie from pie plate, using foil to gently lift.

Cranberry-Peach Tart

Don't be alarmed when the cranberries pop—they have to pop to release natural pectin. Once chilled, the mixture sets and makes cutting easy.

1½ cups all-purpose flour
¼ cup packed brown sugar
⅔ cup margarine or butter, softened
1 egg
2 cans (16 ounces each) sliced peaches in juice, drained and ⅓ cup juice reserved
1½ cups fresh or frozen cranberries
⅔ cup granulated sugar
⅓ cup currants or raisins
1 teaspoon vanilla
¼ teaspoon ground cinnamon

To Complete Recipe:
Whipped cream, if desired

Heat oven to 400°. Mix flour, brown sugar, margarine and egg until dough forms. Press firmly and evenly against bottom and side of ungreased 12-inch pizza pan. Bake 12 to 14 minutes or until golden brown. Cool on wire rack.

Pat peach slices dry with paper towels; cut large peach slices lengthwise in half. Mix reserved peach juice and the cornstarch in 1½ quart saucepan. Stir in the cranberries, granulated sugar and currants. Heat to boiling; reduce heat. Simmer uncovered about 3 minutes, stirring constantly, until cranberry skins pop; remove from heat. Stir in vanilla and cinnamon. Cool 10 minutes. Arrange peach slices on baked crust. Spoon cranberry mixture over peaches. See **To Store** and **To Serve.** *8 servings.*

Per Serving: Calories 370; Protein 4 g; Carbohydrate 56 g (Dietary Fiber 3 g); Fat 16 g (Unsaturated 13 g, Saturated 3 g); Cholesterol 25 mg; Sodium 190 mg. Percent of U.S. RDA: Vitamin A 26%; Vitamin C 4%; Calcium 2%; Iron 8%.

To Store

Refrigerator: Cover tart tightly and refrigerate at least 4 hours but no longer than 48 hours.

To Serve from Refrigerator
Serve with whipped cream.

Cranberry-Peach Tart

Pecan Pie

Don't want to tie up a pie plate in the freezer? Just follow the freezing note for Apple Pie (see page 145).

Pastry for 9-inch One-Crust Pie (see page 149)
⅔ cup sugar
⅓ cup margarine or butter, melted
1 cup dark or light corn syrup
½ teaspoon salt
3 eggs
1 cup pecan halves or broken pecans

To Complete Recipe:
Whipped cream, if desired

Heat oven to 375°. Prepare pastry. Beat sugar, margarine, corn syrup, salt and eggs with hand beater in medium bowl. Stir in pecans. Pour into pastry-lined pie plate. Bake 40 to 50 minutes or until set. STOP HERE—see **To Store** and **To Reheat**.

To complete recipe and serve now, cool slightly on wire rack. Store loosely covered at room temperature no longer than 3 days. Serve warm or cool with whipped cream. *8 servings.*

Per Serving: Calories 530; Protein 5 g; Carbohydrate 63 g (Dietary Fiber 1 g); Fat 29 g (Unsaturated 24 g, Saturated 5 g); Cholesterol 80 mg; Sodium 360 mg. Percent of U.S. RDA: Vitamin A 12%; Vitamin C *; Calcium 2%; Iron 6%.

To Store

Freezer: Cool baked pie on wire rack about 2 hours or until barely warm. Freeze uncovered at least 3 hours until completely frozen. Wrap tightly and label. Freeze no longer than 1 month.

To Reheat from Freezer

About 1 hour before serving, heat oven to 325°. Unwrap pie and bake 45 minutes or until warm. (Place in pie plate if pie was removed from pie plate before freezing.)

Pastry

9-inch One-Crust Pie:
  ⅓ cup plus 1 tablespoon shortening or
    ⅓ cup lard
  1 cup all-purpose flour
  ¼ teaspoon salt
  2 to 3 tablespoons cold water

9-inch Two-Crust Pie:
  ⅔ cup plus 2 tablespoons shortening or
    ⅔ cup lard
  2 cups all-purpose flour
  ½ teaspoon salt
  4 to 5 tablespoons cold water

Cut shortening into flour and salt until particles are size of small peas. Sprinkle in water, 1 tablespoon at a time, tossing with fork until all flour is moistened and pastry almost cleans side of bowl (1 to 2 teaspoons water can be added if necessary).

Gather pastry into a ball. Shape into flattened round on lightly floured surface. (For Two-Crust Pie, divide pastry in half and shape into 2 rounds.) See **TO STORE** and **TO USE.**

To use now, roll pastry 2 inches larger than inverted pie plate, 9 × 1¼ inches, with floured cloth-covered rolling pin. Fold pastry into fourths; place in pie plate. Unfold and ease into plate, pressing firmly against bottom and side.

For One-Crust Pie: Trim overhanging edge of pastry 1 inch from rim of plate. Fold and roll pastry under, even with plate; press with tines of fork or flute if desired. Fill and bake as directed in recipe. *8 servings.*

Per Serving (One Crust): Calories 140; Protein 1 g; Carbohydrate 12 g (Dietary Fiber 0 g); Fat 10 g (Unsaturated 7 g, Saturated 3 g); Cholesterol 0 mg; Sodium 65 mg. Percent of U.S. RDA: Vitamin A *; Vitamin C *; Calcium *; Iron 4%.

For Two-Crust Pie: Turn desired filling into pastry-lined pie plate. Trim overhanging edge of pastry ½ inch from rim of plate. Roll other round of pastry. Fold into fourths and cut slits so steam can escape. Place over filling and unfold. Trim overhanging edge of pastry 1 inch from rim of plate. Fold and roll top edge under lower edge, pressing on rim to seal; press with tines of fork or flute if desired. Bake as directed in recipe. *8 servings.*

Per Serving (Two Crusts): Calories 285; Protein 3 g; Carbohydrate 24 g (Dietary Fiber 1 g); Fat 20 g (Unsaturated 15 g, Saturated 5 g); Cholesterol 0 mg; Sodium 135 mg. Percent of U.S. RDA: Vitamin A *; Vitamin C *; Calcium *; Iron 8%.

TO STORE

Freezer: *Frozen Pastry Circles*: Prepare pastry as directed for Two-Crust Pie. Roll each half of pastry 2 inches larger than inverted pie plate, 9 × 1¼ inches. Stack pastry circles, placing waxed paper between circles, on ungreased cookie sheet. Freeze uncovered 1 hour. Wrap tightly and label. Freeze on flat surface to prevent breaking no longer than 2 months.

TO USE FROM FREEZER

About 25 minutes before using, loosen wrap from circles and let stand at room temperature until soft.

Raspberry-Chocolate Charlotte

This fruit-filled charlotte is also luscious made with apricot liqueur and apricot preserves. When buying ladyfingers, figure on using about one and one half 3-ounce packages. Many ladyfingers come already cut in half, which will save you a step.

> *17 ladyfingers, 3 × 1 × ½ inch*
> *⅓ cup raspberry liqueur, rum or*
>   *raspberry syrup*
> *3 tablespoons water*
> *3 cups whipping (heavy) cream*
> *1 cup hot fudge ice-cream topping*
> *¼ cup raspberry liqueur or*
>   *raspberry syrup*
> *⅔ cup raspberry all-fruit preserves or*
>   *spreadable fruit*

To Complete Recipe:
> *Hot fudge ice-cream topping or whipped*
>   *cream, if desired*

Cut ladyfingers lengthwise in half. Mix ⅓ cup raspberry liqueur and the water. Dip cut surface of each ladyfinger half into liqueur mixture. Arrange ladyfingers, cut sides toward center, on bottom and upright around side of springform pan, 9 × 3 inches. Beat whipping cream in chilled large bowl until stiff. Mix 1 cup hot fudge ice-cream topping and ¼ cup raspberry liqueur; fold into whipped cream.

Spread half of the whipped cream mixture evenly in pan. Spoon half of the preserves by teaspoonfuls onto whipped cream mixture; swirl through preserves and whipped cream mixture with metal spatula or knife. Repeat with remaining whipped cream mixture and preserves. See **To Store** and **To Serve**. *16 servings.*

Per Serving: Calories 300; Protein 2 g; Carbohydrate 28 g (Dietary Fiber 0 g); Fat 20 g (Unsaturated 8 g, Saturated 12 g); Cholesterol 80 mg; Sodium 70 mg. Percent of U.S. RDA: Vitamin A 14%; Vitamin C *; Calcium 6%; Iron 2%.

TO STORE

Freezer: Wrap tightly and label. Freeze at least 6 hours but no longer than 2 months.

TO SERVE FROM FREEZER

About 1 or 2 hours before serving, place wrapped dessert in refrigerator to soften. Loosen side of dessert from pan; remove side of pan. Cut into wedges. Serve with hot fudge topping.

Mini Almond Cheesecakes

Although kids—and adults—love to eat these cheesecakes as snacks on the go, you can also serve them as an elegant dessert. Remove cheesecakes from baking cups and place on dessert plates; drizzle with chocolate sauce. Top with fresh raspberries and a small scoop of raspberry sorbet.

> *12 vanilla wafers*
> *1 package (8 ounces) plus 1 package*
>   *(3 ounces) cream cheese, softened*
> *¼ cup sugar*
> *2 tablespoons amaretto or ½ teaspoon*
>   *almond extract*
> *2 eggs*
> *¼ cup chopped almonds, toasted*

Heat oven to 350°. Line 12 medium muffin cups, 2½ × 1¼ inches, with paper baking cups. Place 1 wafer, flat side down, in each cup. Beat cream cheese and sugar in medium bowl on high speed until fluffy. Beat in amaretto. Beat in eggs, one at a time. Fill cups ¾ full. Sprinkle with almonds. Bake about 20 minutes or until centers are firm. Immediately remove from pan to wire rack. Cool 15 minutes. See **To Store** and **To Serve**. *12 servings.*

Mini Peanut Butter Cheesecakes: Omit almonds. Substitute ½ teaspoon vanilla for the amaretto. Press 1 milk chocolate–covered peanut butter cup (about 1 inch) into cheese mixture in each cup until even with top of cheese mixture. Bake about 15 minutes or until set.

Per Serving: Calories 160; Protein 4 g; Carbohydrate 9 g (Dietary Fiber 0 g); Fat 12 g (Unsaturated 5 g, Saturated 7 g); Cholesterol 65 mg; Sodium 100 mg. Percent of U.S. RDA: Vitamin A 8%; Vitamin C *; Calcium 2%; Iron 4%.

To Store

Refrigerator: Cover and refrigerate at least 2 hours but no longer than 5 days.

Freezer: Refrigerate cheesecakes one hour. Place in labeled airtight freezer container. Freeze no longer than 2 months.

To Serve from Refrigerator

Remove paper baking cups.

To Serve from Freezer

About 2 hours before serving, place wrapped cheesecakes in refrigerator to thaw. Remove paper baking cups.

White Chocolate–Pecan Cheesecake

When melting the vanilla chips, it's important not to mix any water with them, or they will stiffen. If you like, you can melt the vanilla chips in the microwave; follow the manufacturer's directions carefully.

1½ cups graham cracker crumbs (about 20 squares)
¼ cup finely chopped pecans, toasted if desired
⅓ cup margarine or butter, melted
1 cup vanilla milk chips
¾ cup sugar
2 tablespoons all-purpose flour
2 packages (8 ounces each) cream cheese, softened
2 egg yolks
2 eggs
½ cup sour cream

To Complete Recipe:
2 cups cut-up fresh fruit or berries

Move oven rack to lowest position. Heat oven to 400°. Lightly grease springform pan, 8 × 3 inches; remove bottom. Mix graham cracker crumbs, pecans, 2 tablespoons sugar and the margarine. Press about ¾ cup of the crumb mixture evenly on bottom of pan. Place on cookie sheet. Bake 6 to 8 minutes or until golden brown; cool. Assemble bottom and side of pan; secure side. Press remaining crumb mixture 2 inches up side of pan. Cut 11-inch circle of heavy-duty aluminum foil. Place pan on foil circle; press foil up side of pan to prevent dripping in oven during baking.

Place vanilla milk chips in 2-cup heatproof glass measure. Place measure in 1½-quart saucepan. Add water to saucepan until 2 inches deep. Heat over low heat, stirring frequently, until chips are melted. Remove measure from saucepan.

Increase oven temperature to 475°. Beat melted chips, ¾ sugar and the flour in large bowl on medium speed until blended. Beat in cream cheese and egg yolks until smooth. Continue beating, adding the eggs one at a time, then the sour cream until blended. Pour batter carefully into crust. Cover with aluminum foil and bake 20 minutes. Remove foil; reduce oven temperature to 300°. Bake 1 hour. (If cheesecake browns too quickly, cover loosely with aluminum foil during last 30 minutes of baking.)

Turn off oven and leave cheesecake in oven 15 minutes. Remove from oven; cool on wire rack 15 minutes. Run metal spatula along side of cheesecake to loosen before and after refrigerating. STOP HERE—See **TO STORE** and **TO SERVE.** *16 servings.*

Per Serving: Calories 315; Protein 5 g; Carbohydrate 26 g (Dietary Fiber 2 g); Fat 22 g (Unsaturated 11 g, Saturated 11 g); Cholesterol 90 mg; Sodium 190 mg. Percent of U.S. RDA: Vitamin A 16%; Vitamin C 6%; Calcium 4%; Iron 6%.

TO STORE

Refrigerator: Cover tightly and refrigerate at least 8 hours but no longer than 5 days.

Freezer: Wrap tightly and label. Freeze no longer than 4 months.

TO SERVE FROM REFRIGERATOR

Run metal spatula along side of cheesecake to loosen. Remove side of pan; place cheesecake on serving plate. Top with fresh fruit.

TO SERVE FROM FREEZER

About 4 to 6 hours before serving, place wrapped cheesecake in refrigerator to thaw. Run metal spatula along side of cheesecake to loosen. Remove side of pan; place cheesecake on serving plate. Top with fresh fruit.

White Chocolate–Pecan Cheesecake

Crepes Suzette

Crepes (below)
⅔ cup margarine or butter
¾ teaspoon grated orange peel
⅔ cup orange juice
¼ cup sugar

To Complete Recipe:
⅓ cup brandy
⅓ cup orange-flavored liqueur

Prepare Crepes. Heat margarine, orange peel, orange juice and sugar to boiling in 10-inch skillet, stirring occasionally. Boil and stir 1 minute; reduce heat. Fold each crepe into fourths; place in hot orange sauce and turn once. Arrange crepes around edge of skillet. STOP HERE—see **To Store** and **To Reheat.**

To complete recipe and serve now, heat brandy and liqueur in 1-quart saucepan, but do not boil. Pour warm brandy mixture into center of skillet and carefully ignite. Spoon flaming sauce over crepes, using long-handled metal spoon. Serve sauce over crepes. *6 servings.*

CREPES

1½ cups all-purpose flour
1 tablespoon sugar
½ teaspoon salt
2 cups milk
2 tablespoons margarine or butter, melted
½ teaspoon vanilla
2 eggs

Mix flour, sugar and salt in medium bowl. Stir in remaining ingredients. Beat with hand beater until smooth. Lightly grease 6- to 8-inch skillet with margarine or butter; heat over medium heat until bubbly. For each crepe, pour scant ¼ cup of the batter into skillet. *Immediately* rotate skillet until thin film covers bottom. Cook until bottom is light brown. Run wide spatula around edge to loosen; turn and cook other side until light brown. Stack crepes, placing waxed paper between each; keep covered. When removing from skillet, stack so first baked side is down. Cool, keeping crepes covered to prevent them from drying out.

> **Per Serving:** Calories 455; Protein 8 g; Carbohydrate 44 g (Dietary Fiber 1 g); Fat 28 g (Unsaturated 11 g, Saturated 17 g); Cholesterol 140 mg; Sodium 400 mg. Percent of U.S. RDA: Vitamin A 26%; Vitamin C 6%; Calcium 12%; Iron 10%.

TO STORE

Freezer: Refrigerate uncovered 30 minutes. Wrap tightly and label. Freeze no longer than 3 months.

Note: Crepes can be frozen separately no longer than 3 months if desired. To freeze, cool; keep crepes covered to prevent drying out. Make 2 stacks of 6 crepes each, with waxed paper between crepes. Wrap, label and freeze each stack. About 3 hours before serving, remove crepes from freezer and thaw wrapped at room temperature.

TO REHEAT FROM FREEZER

Oven: About 1¼ hours before serving, heat oven to 350°. Bake crepes in covered skillet 40 minutes. Uncover and bake about 20 minutes longer or until hot and bubbly. Heat brandy and liqueur in 1-quart saucepan, but do not boil. Pour warm brandy mixture into center of skillet and carefully ignite. Spoon flaming sauce over crepes, using long-handled metal spoon. Serve sauce over crepes.

Orange-Chocolate Puffs

1 cup water
½ cup (1 stick) margarine or butter
1 cup all-purpose flour
4 eggs
1 teaspoon grated orange peel
Chocolate Glaze (right)
1 cup whipping (heavy) cream
1 tablespoon sugar
1 tablespoon orange-flavored liqueur or
orange juice
1 container (8 ounces) orange yogurt
¼ cup miniature chocolate chips

Heat oven to 400°. Heat water and margarine to rolling boil in 2-quart saucepan. Stir in flour; reduce heat. Stir vigorously over low heat about 1 minute or until mixture forms a ball; remove from heat. Beat in eggs, one at a time, beating until smooth after each addition. Stir in orange peel. Drop dough into 10 mounds onto ungreased cookie sheet.

Bake 35 to 40 minutes or until puffed and golden brown. Cool on cookie sheet away from draft. Prepare Chocolate Glaze. Cut off top one-third of each puff and pull out any filaments of soft dough. Spread Chocolate Glaze over tops of puffs. Let stand until glaze is set.

Beat whipping cream, sugar and liqueur in chilled medium bowl until stiff. Fold in yogurt and chocolate chips. STOP HERE—see **To STORE** and **To SERVE.**

To serve now, fill bottoms of puffs with yogurt mixture; replace tops. *10 servings.*

CHOCOLATE GLAZE

½ cup powdered sugar
2 tablespoons cocoa
3 to 4 teaspoons orange-flavored liqueur
or orange juice

Mix powdered sugar and cocoa. Stir in liqueur, 1 teaspoon at a time, until glaze is spreading consistency.

Per Serving: Calories 340; Protein 5 g; Carbohydrate 31 g (Dietary Fiber 1 g); Fat 22 g (Unsaturated 13 g, Saturated 9 g); Cholesterol 120 mg; Sodium 160 mg. Percent of U.S. RDA: Vitamin A 22%; Vitamin C *; Calcium 6%; Iron 6%.

TO STORE

Refrigerator: Cover yogurt mixture tightly and refrigerate no longer than 24 hours. Cover puffs loosely and store in single layer at room temperature.

Freezer: Fill bottoms of puffs with yogurt mixture; replace tops. Place filled puffs in single layer in labeled airtight freezer container. Freeze no longer than 1 month.

TO SERVE FROM REFRIGERATOR

About 15 minutes before serving, fill bottoms of puffs with yogurt mixture; replace tops.

TO SERVE FROM FREEZER

About 15 minutes before serving, uncover puffs and let stand at room temperature to partially thaw.

Chocolate-Almond Meringues

Want to avoid last-minute assembly? Scoop the ice cream mixture into the meringue shells and freeze the individual servings up to 4 hours ahead. Just before serving, add the whipped cream topping.

> *2 egg whites*
> *¼ teaspoon cream of tartar*
> *½ cup sugar*
> *1 pint chocolate ice cream, slightly softened*
> *½ cup broken chocolate wafers*
> *½ cup slivered almonds, toasted*
> *2 tablespoons crème de cacao or milk*

To Complete Recipe:
> *½ cup whipping (heavy) cream*
> *1 tablespoon crème de cacao*
> *Chocolate curls or shaved chocolate, if desired*

Heat oven to 275°. Cover cookie sheet with cooking parchment paper or aluminum foil. Beat egg whites and cream of tartar in medium bowl on medium speed until foamy. Beat in sugar, 1 tablespoon at a time; continue beating until stiff and glossy. Do not underbeat. Drop meringue by ⅓ cupfuls onto paper. Shape into 3-inch circles, building up sides. Bake 1 hour. Turn off oven and leave meringues in oven with door closed 1½ hours. Finish cooling meringues at room temperature.

Mix ice cream, chocolate wafers, almonds and 2 tablespoons crème de cacao. Cover and freeze at least 1 hour. STOP HERE—see **To Store** and **To Serve.**

To complete recipe and serve now, beat whipping cream and 1 tablespoon crème de cacao in chilled medium bowl until stiff. Divide ice cream mixture among meringue shells. Top with whipped cream and chocolate curls. *6 servings.*

Per Serving: Calories 350; Protein 6 g; Carbohydrate 40 g (Dietary Fiber 1 g); Fat 19 g (Unsaturated 10 g, Saturated 9 g); Cholesterol 45 mg; Sodium 150 mg. Percent of U.S. RDA: Vitamin A 10%; Vitamin C *; Calcium 10%; Iron 6%.

TO STORE

Freezer: Place cooled meringue shells in labeled airtight freezer container. Freeze meringues and ice cream mixture no longer than 1 month.

TO SERVE FROM FREEZER

Beat whipping cream and 1 tablespoon crème de cacao in chilled medium bowl until stiff. Divide ice cream mixture among meringue shells. Top with whipped cream and chocolate curls.

Chocolate-Almond Meringues

Three-Nut Baklava

To toast nuts, sprinkle them in an ungreased heavy 10-inch skillet. Cook over medium heat 5 to 7 minutes, stirring frequently, until nuts begin to brown, then stirring constantly until light brown. Nuts will continue to darken after they are removed from the heat.

1 cup (2 sticks) margarine or butter, melted
1 cup finely chopped walnuts, toasted
½ cup sliced almonds, toasted
½ cup finely chopped macadamia nuts, toasted
½ cup flaked coconut
2 tablespoons sugar
½ teaspoon ground allspice
1 package (16 ounces) frozen phyllo sheets (18 × 14 inches), thawed
1¼ cups water
¾ cup sugar
3 tablespoons honey
1 tablespoon lemon juice

To Complete Recipe:
Unsweetened whipped cream, if desired

Heat oven to 350°. Brush bottom and sides of rectangular pan, 13 × 9 × 2 inches, generously with some of the margarine. Mix walnuts, almonds, macadamia nuts, coconut, 2 table-spoons sugar and the allspice.

While working with phyllo, cover with plastic wrap, then with damp towel to prevent sheets from drying out. Brush and layer 15 sheets phyllo lightly with margarine. Cut stack cross-wise in half into 2 rectangles, 14 × 9 inches. Place half of the stack in pan, folding edges to fit pan if necessary. Sprinkle half of the nut mixture over phyllo. Top with remaining stack. Sprinkle with remaining nut mixture. Brush and layer remaining phyllo sheets lightly with margarine. Cut stack crosswise in half, then place both stacks on nuts; press lightly.

Cut phyllo about ½ inch deep into 5 lengthwise strips, about 1½ inches wide. Make diagonal cuts across strips, ½ inch deep and about 1¼ inches wide, to make diamond shapes. Bake about 35 minutes or until phyllo is golden brown.

Heat water, ¾ cup sugar and the honey to boiling in 1½-quart saucepan, stirring occasionally; reduce heat. Simmer uncovered 10 minutes. Stir in lemon juice. Pour hot mixture over warm phyllo. Cut along scored lines to bottom. Cool completely. See **To Store** and **To Serve.**

To complete recipe and serve now, top each serving with whipped cream. *36 pieces.*

Per Piece: Calories 150; Protein 2 g; Carbohydrate 16 g (Dietary Fiber 1 g); Fat 9 g (Unsaturated 7 g, Saturated 2 g); Cholesterol 0 mg; Sodium 105 mg. Percent of U.S. RDA: Vitamin A 6%; Vitamin C *; Calcium *; Iron 4%.

TO STORE

Freezer: Wrap cooled baklava in pan tightly and label. Freeze no longer than 2 months.

TO SERVE FROM FREEZER

About 3 hours before serving, unwrap baklava and let stand at room temperature to thaw. Top each serving with whipped cream.

Three-Nut Baklava

Date-Rice Pudding

2 cups milk
½ cup uncooked regular long grain rice
½ cup chopped dates
½ cup half-and-half
2 tablespoons sugar
1 teaspoon vanilla
½ teaspoon grated orange peel
¼ teaspoon ground cinnamon

Heat milk and rice just to boiling in 2-quart saucepan over medium heat; reduce heat. Cover and simmer 30 to 40 minutes, stirring occasionally, until most of the milk is absorbed. Stir in remaining ingredients. See **TO STORE** and **TO SERVE**. *4 servings, about ½ cup each.*

Per Serving: Calories 280; Protein 7 g; Carbohydrate 50 g (Dietary Fiber 1 g); Fat 6 g (Unsaturated 2 g, Saturated 4 g); Cholesterol 20 mg; Sodium 75 mg. Percent of U.S. RDA: Vitamin A 10%; Vitamin C *; Calcium 20%; Iron 6%.

TO STORE

Refrigerator: Refrigerate tightly covered at least 4 hours but no longer than 48 hours.

TO SERVE FROM REFRIGERATOR

Serve with whipped cream if desired.

Chocolate Chip–Peanut Frozen Yogurt

These chocolate- and peanut-studded treats are perfect for children's parties, without the mess and fuss of individual scoops of ice cream for each child.

3 containers (8 ounces each) vanilla
    yogurt
¼ cup miniature semisweet chocolate
    chips
¼ cup chopped honey-roasted peanuts
2 tablespoons honey

Mix all ingredients. Pour into loaf pan, 8½ × 4½ × 2½ or 9 × 5 × 3 inches. Cover tightly and freeze 4 to 6 hours or until firm. Cut yogurt mixture into chunks and place in chilled bowl. Beat on low speed until no large pieces remain. Divide among 10 foil baking cups, 2½ inches in diameter. See **TO STORE** and **TO SERVE**. *8 servings, about ½ cup each.*

Per Serving: Calories 160; Protein 5 g; Carbohydrate 25 g (Dietary Fiber 1 g); Fat 5 g (Unsaturated 3 g, Saturated 2 g); Cholesterol 5 mg; Sodium 80 mg. Percent of U.S. RDA: Vitamin A *; Vitamin C *; Calcium 14%; Iron 2%.

TO STORE

Freezer: Place cups in single layer in labeled airtight freezer container. Freeze no longer than 1 month.

TO SERVE FROM FREEZER

Serve in baking cups or remove cups before serving.

Chocolate Chip–Peanut Frozen Yogurt

Sherried Fruit Compote

1 cup dried apricots
1¾ cups pear nectar
¾ cup cream sherry, or 2 teaspoons
  sherry extract plus ⅔ cup apple juice
½ teaspoon ground allspice
½ teaspoon ground cardamom
⅛ teaspoon ground cloves
1 cup seedless red grapes, cut in half
2 medium pears, sliced

To Complete Recipe:
½ cup lemon or orange yogurt

Mix apricots, pear nectar, sherry, allspice, cardamom and cloves in 1-quart saucepan. Heat to boiling; reduce heat. Simmer uncovered 5 minutes; cool. Stir in grapes and pears; cool. STOP HERE—see **To Store** and **To Serve.**

To complete recipe and serve now, top each serving with yogurt. *6 servings, about ⅔ cup each.*

Per Serving: Calories 175; Protein 2 g; Carbohydrate 44 g (Dietary Fiber 4 g); Fat 1 g (Unsaturated 1 g, Saturated 0 g); Cholesterol 2 mg; Sodium 20 mg. Percent of U.S. RDA: Vitamin A 18%; Vitamin C 8%; Calcium 6%; Iron 8%.

To Store

Refrigerator: Refrigerate tightly covered no longer than 2 weeks.

To Serve from Refrigerator

Top each serving with yogurt.

Plum-Pear Sorbet

Use the apricot nectar for a sweeter flavor.

2 cans (16 ounces each) plums, drained
  and pitted
1 cup pear or apricot nectar
¼ cup sugar
1 teaspoon vanilla

Place all ingredients in blender or food processor. Cover and blend, or process, about 15 seconds or until smooth. Pour into loaf pan, 8½ × 4½ × 2½ inches. See **To Store** and **To Serve.** *4 servings, about ½ cup each.*

Per Serving: Calories 230; Protein 1 g; Carbohydrate 60 g (Dietary Fiber 4 g); Fat 0 g (Unsaturated 0 g, Saturated 0 g); Cholesterol 0 mg; Sodium 35 mg. Percent of U.S. RDA: Vitamin A 6%; Vitamin C *; Calcium 2%; Iron 8%.

To Store

Freezer: Cover tightly and freeze at least 24 hours but no longer than 1 month.

To Serve from Freezer

Scrape ice cream scoop or spoon about ½ inch deep across top of sorbet, and mound into dessert dishes.

⊠⊠⊠ Guidelines for ⊠⊠⊠ Cold Storage

We've come a long way from the ice box and the ice delivery man. It seems that modern refrigerators and freezers should be able to keep foods forever—but they can't! Below are some pointers and a time chart to help you keep foods safely stored in both the refrigerator and freezer. We recommend that you purchase a refrigerator/freezer thermometer and check it often to make sure the correct temperatures are being maintained.

Refrigerator

- Keep the refrigerator temperature at 40° F. or slightly lower. Adjust the temperature to a colder setting after prolonged exposure to room temperature or when warm foods are added. The temperature can be readjusted to the normal setting after about 8 hours.
- Use the times given in the chart for refrigerating foods. They may seem short but will help keep foods from spoiling or becoming dangerous to eat. (See Tips for Safe Food Handling, page 13.)
- Cover foods or close original containers tightly before refrigerating to prevent drying out or transfer of odors to or from other foods. Store produce and strong-flavored foods in tightly covered containers or plastic bags to retain moisture.
- Remove foods from the refrigerator just before you are ready to use them.

Freezer

- Keep freezer temperature at 0° F. or slightly lower.
- Wrap food in moistureproof, vaporproof containers and materials. (See Wrap It Up!, page 10.)
- Label and date all packages and containers.
- Remove as much air from packages as possible to prevent freezer burn (see Airtight Is Right!, page 8).
- Keep purchased frozen foods in the original packages.
- Use longest-stored foods first.
- Always thaw frozen meats, poultry and seafood in the refrigerator or use the microwave; never allow them to stand at room temperature. Allow about 5 hours for each pound.
- Use the times given for freezing foods to maintain best flavor and texture. Frozen foods kept slightly longer are still safe to eat.

HELPFUL TIPS AND SPECIAL DIRECTIONS

Baked Products: Cool completely before wrapping airtight for freezing. Allow frostings to harden or freeze uncovered *before* packaging.

Breads: Refrigerate only during hot, humid weather in original packaging. Loosen wrap and thaw frozen bread at room temperature 2 to 3 hours.

Cakes: Refrigerate cakes with custard or whipped cream filling or frosting. Loosen wrap on frozen unfrosted cakes and thaw at room temperature 2 to 3 hours. Loosen wrap on frozen frosted cakes and thaw overnight in refrigerator.

Cheesecakes: Thaw wrapped in refrigerator 4 to 6 hours.

Cookies: Freeze delicate or frosted and decorated cookies in single layers separated by waxed paper. Thaw covered in container at room temperature 1 to 2 hours. Crisp-textured cookies should be removed from container to thaw.

Pies: *Frozen unbaked fruit pies:* Unwrap and carefully cut slits in top crust. Bake at 425° for 15 minutes. Reduce heat to 375° and bake 30 to 45 minutes longer or until crust is golden brown and juice begins to bubble through slits.

Frozen baked fruit and pecan pies: Unwrap and thaw at room temperature until completely thawed. Or unwrap and thaw at room temperature 1 hour, then heat in 375° oven for 35 to 40 minutes or until warm. Unwrap and thaw baked pumpkin pies in refrigerator.

Dairy Products: Check package for the freshness date and refrigerate in original containers. Refrigeration time is for *opened* products.

Cream Cheese and Hard Cheese: If hard cheese is moldy, trim ½ inch from affected area and replace wrap each time. Thaw frozen cheeses wrapped in refrigerator. Use only in baked goods due to texture changes.

Ice Cream, Sorbet, Frozen Yogurt: Freeze in original container. Cover surface directly with aluminum foil or plastic wrap to reduce ice crystals. For best quality, do not thaw and refreeze.

Whipped Cream: Freeze in small mounds on waxed paper until firm, then place in airtight container.

Eggs: To refrigerate yolks only, cover with cold water and refrigerate tightly covered. To freeze eggs, add ⅛ teaspoon salt or ½ teaspoon sugar for every 4 yolks or 2 whole eggs and freeze tightly covered.

Meat Products: Check packages for the freshness date. Refrigerate or freeze meat in the original package, as repeated handling can introduce bacteria to meat and poultry. Overwrap with heavy-duty aluminum foil or freezer wrap, or place in freezer bags for freezing.

COLD STORAGE CHART

FOODS	REFRIGERATOR (34° TO 40°F.)	FREEZER (0°F. OR BELOW)
Baked Products		
Breads—coffee cakes, muffins, quick breads and yeast breads	5 to 7 days	2 to 3 months
Cakes—unfrosted and frosted	3 to 5 days	Unfrosted—3 to 4 months Frosted—2 to 3 months
Cheesecakes—baked	3 to 5 days	4 to 5 months
Cookies—baked	No need to refrigerate unless stated in recipe	Unfrosted—No longer than 12 months Frosted—No longer than 3 months
Pies—unbaked or baked baked pecan and baked pumpkin pies	Baked pumpkin pies 3 to 5 days Store fresh fruit or baked fruit pies and baked pecan pies loosely covered at room temperature no longer than 3 days	*Unbaked fruit pies* 2 to 3 months *Baked pies* 3 to 4 months
Pie shells—unbaked or baked	Store in freezer	*Unbaked shells* no longer than 2 months *Baked shells* no longer than 4 months
Dairy Products		
Cheese •Cottage and ricotta	1 to 10 days	Not recommended
•Cream	No longer than 2 weeks	No longer than 2 months
•Hard	3 to 4 weeks	6 to 8 weeks
Ice Cream, Sorbet and Frozen Yogurt	Freeze only	2 to 4 months

(continued on following pages)

COLD STORAGE CHART (*continued*)

Milk Products		
Buttermilk	No longer than 1 week	Not recommended
Cream, half-and-half and whipping	No longer than 5 days	Not recommended
Cream, whipped	1 to 2 days	No longer than 3 months
Regular milk, whole, 2%, 1% and skim	No longer than 5 days	No longer than 1 month
Sour cream	No longer than 1 week	Not recommended
Yogurt	No longer than 3 weeks	No longer than 1 month
Eggs		
Raw •Whole in shell •Raw yolks, whites	3 weeks 2 to 4 days Cover yolks with cold water	Not recommended No longer than 12 months See **Eggs**, page 164
Cooked •Whole in shell •Yolks, whites	1 week 1 week	Not recommended Don't freeze well
Fats and Oils		
Butter	No longer than 2 weeks	No longer than 2 months
Margarine	No longer than 1 month	No longer than 2 months
Mayonnaise and salad dressing	No longer than 6 months	Not recommended
Meat		
Meats—Uncooked Chops Ground Roasts and Steaks	3 to 5 days 1 to 2 days 3 to 5 days	4 to 6 months 3 to 4 months 6 to 12 months

Meats—Cooked	3 to 4 days	2 to 3 months
Meats—Processed Cold Cuts	3 to 5 days 2 weeks, unopened	Not recommended
Cured Bacon	5 to 7 days	No longer than 1 month
Franks	1 week; 2 weeks, unopened	1 to 2 months
Ham •Canned, unopened •Whole or half, fully cooked •Slices, fully cooked	6 to 9 months 5 to 7 days 3 to 4 days	Not recommended 1 to 2 months 1 to 2 months
Poultry		
Poultry—Uncooked •Whole (including game birds, ducks and geese) •Cut up •Giblets	1 to 2 days 1 to 2 days 1 to 2 days	No longer than 12 months No longer than 9 months No longer than 3 months
Poultry—Cooked	3 to 4 days	4 months
Seafood		
Fin Fish •Uncooked fatty fish (mackerel, salmon, trout, tuna, etc.) •Uncooked lean fish (cod, flounder, grouper, halibut, orange roughy, red snapper, scrod, etc.) •Cooked and breaded	1 to 2 days 1 to 2 days Store in freezer	2 to 3 months 4 to 6 months 2 to 3 months
Shellfish •Uncooked •Cooked	1 to 2 days 3 to 4 days	3 to 4 months

METRIC CONVERSION GUIDE

U.S. UNITS	CANADIAN METRIC	AUSTRALIAN METRIC
Volume		
1/4 teaspoon	1 mL	1 ml
1/2 teaspoon	2 mL	2 ml
1 teaspoon	5 mL	5 ml
1 tablespoon	15 mL	20 ml
1/4 cup	50 mL	60 ml
1/3 cup	75 mL	80 ml
1/2 cup	125 mL	125 ml
2/3 cup	150 mL	170 ml
3/4 cup	175 mL	190 ml
1 cup	250 mL	250 ml
1 quart	1 liter	1 liter
1 1/2 quarts	1.5 liter	1.5 liter
2 quarts	2 liters	2 liters
2 1/2 quarts	2.5 liters	2.5 liters
3 quarts	3 liters	3 liters
4 quarts	4 liters	4 liters
Weight		
1 ounce	30 grams	30 grams
2 ounces	55 grams	60 grams
3 ounces	85 grams	90 grams
4 ounces (1/4 pound)	115 grams	125 grams
8 ounces (1/2 pound)	225 grams	225 grams
16 ounces (1 pound)	455 grams	500 grams
1 pound	455 grams	1/2 kilogram

Measurements		Temperatures	
Inches	Centimeters	Fahrenheit	Celsius
1	2.5	32°	0°
2	5.0	212°	100°
3	7.5	250°	120°
4	10.0	275°	140°
5	12.5	300°	150°
6	15.0	325°	160°
7	17.5	350°	180°
8	20.5	375°	190°
9	23.0	400°	200°
10	25.5	425°	220°
11	28.0	450°	230°
12	30.5	475°	240°
13	33.0	500°	260°
14	35.5		
15	38.0		

NOTE
The recipes in this cookbook have not been developed or tested using metric measures. When converting recipes to metric, some variations in quality may be noted.

✄✄✄ Index ✄✄✄

Numbers in *italics* refer to illustrations.

75 POINTS

SAVE these Betty Crocker Points and redeem them for big savings on hundreds of kitchen, home, gift and children's items! For catalog, send 50¢ with your name and address to: General Mills, P.O. Box 5389, Mpls., MN 55460.

Redeemable with cash in USA before May 1999. Void where prohibited, taxed or regulated.

S

CUT OUT AND SAVE